Mind Is Too Mental

As

Teeth Are Too Dental

And We All Have A Mind…

Evadynè Smith

Read Along

Mind Is Too Mental As Teeth Are Too Dental

You Dream and Then You Live Your Dreams…

Mind Is Too Mental As Teeth Are Too Dental

Published in the United States by Evadynè Smith

Printing by KindleDirectPublishing Inc.

ISBN: 979-8-3697-16427

Mind Is Too Mental As Teeth Are Too Dental

We are always becoming ourselves so there are no mistakes; it
is all in the process of becoming....

Mind Is Too Mental As Teeth Are Too Dental

Table of Contents

Mind Is Too Mental As Teeth Are Too Dental

I humbly ask our Creator to please protect our minds, bodies, hearts, souls, and spirits to be able to sustain good health and wellness.

To please give us the strength and the ability to reach out and talk to someone about our feelings, when not feeling good.

I ask that we not be afraid to share life's lessons, good and not so good, so that our experiences can be a benefit to others.

I ask that we take the time to record or write down our feelings, as a way of clearing our minds and our souls, so that our bodies can remain whole.

I ask this for all humans and humankind alike.

Thank You

Evadynè

Dedication

To Everyone who reads or listens to this book.

We have a right to know and understand our bodies, from head to toe.

We are powerful, when connected, like electrical extension cords.

So, let's learn more, to be more, and have more of what we deserve…

A happy and completely healthy, whole life, including…

"Above The Chin!"

I dedicate this book to

You, Me, We, Thee, Thou!

Evadyne

Mind Is Too Mental As Teeth Are Too Dental

This book is meant to provide a basic understanding of one of the most devasting actions of a not so good mind/mental condition.

It will share about other conditions that cause lifelong challenging events.

It will help bring an understanding to, what we choose and what we know about, what we are choosing.

In layman terms, using basic words, giving food for thought, directing to search for more answers by using the world wide web (www), the internet (connection of the satellites), to get a better understanding, that may fit into your life.

Mind/mental health conditions are long term, life changing, and generational.

Mind/mental health includes being happy, excited, enthusiastic, inspirational, great mood, good mood, not so good and in need of assistance.

The best mind/mental health condition can change in a flash, and if we don't know the how, and why....it can get worse.

It can also be a gradual change.

Mind Is Too Mental As Teeth Are Too Dental

A person's personality may be deepening in actions, and we say, "oh that's how they have always been."

But pay close attention to them, because the "always been", can be bending further in the wrong direction.

Be mindful and try not to ignore the signs of progressive mind deterioration.

Know that "it's not just you, or me or our family members and friends", who may be experiencing these conditions, it is all over the world.

Mind is too mental as teeth are too dental, and we all have a mind. Right?

We, my co-Author and I are just putting forth our efforts to make this world a better place, one human at a time.

My co-Author is My Creator.

Thank You For Understanding.

Evadynè

Mind Is Too Mental As Teeth Are Too Dental

Always Remember That Joy Begins With Nature...

It's All Around Us...

It Reigns With Opportunities For More....

Mind Is Too Mental As Teeth Are Too Dental

Foreword

Mind is too mental as teeth are too dental, makes a whole lot of sense. Right? And we all have a mind. Right?

It is the state of our minds that the mental department gets assigned to figure out. I call it; "above the chin".

Mental health speaks about the condition of our thoughts and actions within our heads, that ultimately affect the other parts of our bodies, and the outside world as well.

This title came to me, when I was thinking that the information between these covers is very important, but people were afraid of the word suicide. They stayed away from learning and understanding how and why people take their own lives. They judge them and don't care to understand the real causes, or if even, it was a self-inflicted cause.

So, I needed something softer, and remembering the expressions on people's faces when I made that statement above, it was like…. Yeah, I got it…so there we have it. Fear not, the knowledge that will set you free.

Mind is Too Mental as Teeth are Too Dental and We All Have a Mind!

Mind Is Too Mental As Teeth Are Too Dental

Contact the National Suicide and Crisis Lifeline

Text or Dial 988

Veterans and Active Military Preventing Substance Abuse and Suicide: https://www.linesforlife.org/mhl/ or

Text 838255

The deaf and hard of hearing can contact the Lifeline via TTY.

Dial 711

http://www.suicidepreventionlifeline.org/
GetHelp/LifelineChat.aspx

Suicide Prevention Resource Guide

http://www.sprc.org/resources-programs/program-
encourageactive-rewarding-lives-pearls

Association of Black Psychologists

http://www.abpsi.org/find-psychologists

Association of Psychiatry

www.Psychiatry.org

Mind Is Too Mental As Teeth Are Too Dental

Mind Is Too Mental, As Teeth Are Too Dental…

Monumental!

Heal the hurt. Heal the pain.

Don't let the darkness remain.

Be safe! Be sane! Don't let the ugly maintain!

Time is your friend, it's not the end!

You can regroup and win!

Do the work, reverse the hurts, and reap the perks.

Take charge! Make the change! Self-Affirm!

You have the mind. You have the mental!

It's not Incidental!

Stand Up and Be A Winner!

Written with Care and Submitted By

Deborah Fitzgerald

6/17/2023

Mind Is Too Mental As Teeth Are Too Dental

Let's Begin...

Preface

As we think about mind/mental health, the most extreme, unspoken, hush, hush, action that most people associate mind/mental health with, is suicide.

The most untrue statement used most often when a person attempts or completes any act of self-harm, includes "they must have been suffering in silence" or "you never know who is suffering in silence". I feel those words are a "loud" misstatement, and a way for people to come to terms with the action. The lack of understanding, the who, what, where, when, how and why, keeps us in such darkness about the how easily this can occur with anyone. How this can happen to happy, successful, young, or our elders, at any time.

After you read this book, you may agree with me that "they may not have been suffering at all". That the act could have been the result of something as natural as protein deficiency, or the side effects of medications. They do mention that in the commercials…right?

In this book, I first want to demystifying suicide by identifying some of its causes. This will help to bring an understanding and

Mind Is Too Mental As Teeth Are Too Dental

help to remove many of the stigmas associated with the word, "suicide". Understanding will help put a stop to this agent, and that is the goal.

Feeling sad and lonely...with no hope in sight? That is how most people feel about the victims of this agent called suicide. Loved ones can only guess what was going on in the persons mind and life at the time they decided to end it.

There are victims of this agent that gave it much thought and attention. They took the time to create a plan of when and how. Some wrote notes or made a call and of course some did neither of the above. However, the acts that allowed this agent to win required actions thinking and finally a decision. But not necessarily by the victims` own will.

In some cases, it was a quick thought, then action with no preexisting conditions of emotional distress, sadness, or feelings of hopelessness. In fact, it was chemical imbalances, nutritional deficiencies, mind manipulation, side effects of medications, bad advice, or possibly the result of alcohol abuse or street drugs. The reality of these causes are more common than we know. Many people are not thinking about these options at all. Although we hear the commercial warnings for the possible side effects of medications; "may cause sadness, depression and suicidal thoughts," we never think about what those feelings and thoughts would sound like. These same effects can cause homicidal thoughts as well. But more importantly, the commercials do not include information about how those feelings might appear or what those thoughts would sound like, so that we may be more prepared to guard and protect ourselves and others.

So how are we to know? Who is explaining why and how the medication can cause these effects in the body? Well one thing is, it could decrease our protein levels, which would cause our neurotransmitters to not function properly. This chemical change could result in having confusing thoughts, sad thinking, hopelessness, and end of life thinking. These thoughts can come quickly or over time.

Let us see how we can change some of these actions. What can we do to better arm ourselves and others against its attack? How can we make sure that we have good protein levels daily, especially when taking medications or engaging in activities that may decrease our protein levels. We can start with using quality protein, products, nutritional supplements including protein powders, protein bars and through our direct natural food sources.

Let us also start using one of the most powerful weapons against it. The one that will cause its demise. The one that will stop it in its tracks. Knowledge is powerful and it can bring forth a better understanding of all things. Let's start with…

Communication!

Is it that easy you ask? Well just continue reading and we will see!

Here are two examples of what I knew was possible.

A very Gentle Man shared a story with me. He was riding on a bus one day and was approached by a young lady who said, "Hi, do you remember me?" He answered, "No." She explained to him that one evening while she was passing by him, he spoke to her "Wishing her a good evening". They talked for a while. She explained to him that on that day, she was on her way to end her life, but their talk changed her mind.

A simple act of him being kind and gentle, as he always is, and allowing himself to be used by the Higher Power in the way that he is most comfortable. This natural occurrence allowed for a life to be saved. He is not a practicing Psychiatrist,

Psychologist, Social Worker, or Mental Health professional.
He is however a Human Being, doing the best that he could, at
being just that.

The other example that I heard was while watching a video that
Mr. Bryan Sharpe shared: The Founder of the Happiness
Project Mr. E. was explaining his campaign to spread
happiness. His approach would be "Hi may I have 30 seconds
of your time?" Followed by the question "On a scale of 1–10
what level of happiness is your life at?" He tells a story of
when he came across a young man who did not have the 30
seconds for the question. The young man responded with; "No
and no again." Long story short they spoke for about 30
minutes after which the young man asked for Mr. E.'s name.

Although, he usually did not give his name, he told him
anyway. The young man called Mr. E after researching him
and finding his number. He told him that on the day they met
he was planning to commit suicide and that Mr. E. changed his
life with their talk.

Ironically, I met Mr. E. some years prior to watching the video
he asked me that same question, and my response was "Is 10
the highest"? Life is but a dream so live it.

Mind Is Too Mental As Teeth Are Too Dental

Imagine how these two gentlemen must have felt hearing these confessions. Confession is really good for the soul!

What these examples teaches are two lessons:

We must know that our Creator will answer all requests. Keep yourself positioned to hear, see and feel the answers and sometimes that means getting out of our own way, and that we can be valuable to each other doing what we naturally do. Working together for the greater good and wellness of all.

Realizing that the payment for this type of work cannot be spent, and that is okay. Therefore, you could never go broke of the joy that you will feel by knowing, even without confessions, that you have been a great help to someone else.

These are just a couple of examples. I am sure there are more. You may even know some stories where such random encounters or good conversations changed the path of a person's life. Share them with us, if you would like to.

Some of us have no idea of the positive effect that we can have on someone's life.

Then some of us do have an idea and are happy to know that it is possible!

Be with positive purpose in all that you do.

Make a positive purposeful difference in someone's life today and every day.

It will positively affect yours.

Mind Is Too Mental As Teeth Are Too Dental

Please read this book with an open mind!

This book is not meant to be the end all solution for everyone or the one and only answer. However, it is meant to be a part of the solution process. One more tool that will lead to lives being saved and positively changed for the betterment of all. It should also start conversations about a subject that many want to keep "hush, hush". When I say you, us, and we through these pages I am referring to those who will be empowered, inspired, and motivated by these words and who will share them.

There are several reasons that could lead people to have thoughts, make attempts and complete the act of suicide. These reasons could be from emotional disorders, present situations or as we will see, chemical imbalances. Sometimes there are no signs because there were no pre-existing issues. So, for all of you, who have lost a loved one, know that you may have not missed any signs at all. Chemical imbalances caused by different sources, as you will read in these pages, may not have shown any noticeable signs in a person's life. It could be an instant thought followed by an action. Especially if they were living a happy and fulfilled life. Watch: "13 Reason Why". Now let's explore understand and end this together.

Mind Is Too Mental As Teeth Are Too Dental

Please know that we all are powerful and full of gifts that have been given to us to use.

Know that once we realize our special reasons for being here, our lives can become fuller richer and happier.

Before us, within our reach, is all that we need to fulfill the destiny that each one of us have been given.

Stay clear minded, keeping before you and around you what and who helps to nourish your soul and your spirit.

All of which can help you and where your strengths grow, and your energy rejuvenates.

Evadynè

Mind Is Too Mental As Teeth Are Too Dental

Please keep your hearts and minds clear. Do not panic or allow feelings of anxiety to take away your joys and times of happiness. Remember that changes in life happen every day. If you have loved ones, love them, and let them know. Stay in touch and have no regrets. We lose loved ones every day. Some with and some without warning. So, record videos and audios of your conversations with your loved ones, so that they never really leave you. You will always be able to pull up footage and see their smiles, hear their laughter, and feel good about their life, that you shared, then you share it with all of your family. Sharing is Caring.

Being prepared for passing on, makes it easier to live on. Start putting your affairs in order. This will help the process for your loved ones at that time. Also, everyone 18 years or older, unmarried, your child or not, needs a Healthcare Proxy form completed. If not, the state will have the last say on their care.

So, stay up and keep your head high. Laugh and eat, and play, and dance and use the internet to stay in touch, while you laugh, and eat and play and dance. We cannot control everything that happens on the outside, but we can control how we handle it on the inside. Stay Awake and Stay Aware!

Chapter 1

Profile of These Agents

The "agents" are anything that challenges a healthy mind/mental state. From suicide to self-harm, to depression, to Alzheimer's, to ADHD and the various personality disorders, diagnosed or undiagnosed. A healthy mind/mental state is important.

This agent has no real relationship with its victims. However, there are commonalities among some of them. In these cases, the victims may have financial hardships, or they may have a personality that does not allow them to get along well with others. They may not be understood by the people that are around them. There are those that have been abused verbally, physically, mentally, emotionally, academically, or professionally. Others that may have physical, emotional, mental or mind disabilities because of chemical imbalances. Some may have been victims of crimes such as social crimes against humanity, discrimination, humiliation, rape, bullying, or could be a victim of a deaf ear; having no one who is really listening to them. Then again, none of these may be the case as these pages will reveal to you.

Suicide this agent takes its time and breaks down every single opportunity that it finds with its victims. There is so much power in words and so often people use words to harm others directly. This harm can also be an indirect action, such as others speaking about you or on your behalf, who may not understand you at all. Therefore, their perspective of you, is what will be translated to the next person, which can harm you, just by what they are saying, from their personal perspectives on life.

You may have people speaking about you or on your behalf, to individuals who may be in position to determine your resources and your success. This can cause problems for you, and you are not even aware that these conversations are happening. The results will show, but you will not know the root of the new issues that you may be faced with in the future. People concern themselves with "curse words" as being a form of abuse, and that is not always the case. Words of threat and fear can cause more harm than "curse words" ever could. Choosing your words wisely is so important. Adults should not talk around children negatively about their adult relationships.

Using words that are degrading and talking down about a person that the child may love and care about. This type of talk can make the child have ill and untrusting feelings about the person who is being put down. As children grow up with these conversations in their minds and with these ill feelings in their hearts, the child cannot trust the speaker, nor can they trust the one being spoken about, after the stories they have heard. So here is another opportunity for this agent to enter, lay low and grow more and more, until an opportune time to pop up.

The effect of this on the child can be no hope, nowhere to turn, no one to talk to, about the bully in school, about the sexual abuse, about the sex, drugs and alcohol that are being introduced to them by anyone. There is no "out", for this young potential victim and here, in this hole of emptiness, pain and confusion is where this agent finds an opportunity to plant itself and bloom. Popping in and out like a jumping bean. In full sight of the inner soul of this potential young victim. Now this person may still be a child or teen or may have grown into an adult with these underlying, deep, unresolved issues. As life goes on, this agent hides deep in the subconscious of its potential victim waiting for a weak time to attack. It preys on people who, for a short time may lose control of their thinking.

Some people begin to doubt themselves and those around them, which can leave an open door or window for this sneaky sneak to creep in. Some victims engage in activities that alter their thinking. Be it substances, organizational meetings, bad company, professional encounters or dealing with other entities who are trusted, but who are not clear in their own mental/mind space.

These situations can allow weakness of thought and self-control. This agent is happy to find a new place to plant itself. It patiently waits to grow or may find an opportunity to attack. Once inside, this sneaky sneak imbeds itself into the thinking zone of the targeted victim. Lying dormant, while growing and waiting for the right time to strike. That is the plan. It knows its victim's joys and is happy for their pains. It is sneaky. It is weak. That's why it is harder for it to win when it attacks someone who is at their strongest and at their most awake and aware time.

The most opportune time for it to strike is when all heck is breaking loose. Loss of a spouse or mate, loss of a child, loss of any loved one. Loss of a job or faced with a repercussion of a voluntary or involuntary act. The loss of a relationship can be a critical time for a person if they have relied on their partner for their own happiness and stability. Now this thing is full grown and knocking on the conscious mind asking to be let out. It is ready to play with all that it knows to be your weak spots. Don't open the door. Don't let it in. Do not give it a place to perform.

Do know that life goes on after a breakup. Find your happiness within yourself. Bring that happiness to the relationship and never lose it, no matter what happens. Watch How to Have Happy Relationship on YouTube.com/@evadynesmith3986

This agent is sneaky. It has watched and listened to your deepest desires. It has been there for a long time. It feels familiar like lyrics of music, themes of movies and video games. Familiar and comfortable to you because it has become a part of you. Well shake it off when it pops in, to attack. Take control of your future. Keep your happy thoughts near so that you can get to them quickly.

Mind Is Too Mental As Teeth Are Too Dental

Do not let this agent get the best of you, now that you know how it looks, and how it creeps in. You must…BE AWARE and BE STRONG to win this fight. Stay strong, that's the key. Staying aware and awake makes you powerful. Being prepared for the unwelcomed possibility of loss and being ready to start over. The key is to keep living with what you know is good.

If you are feeling that familiar feeling, that maybe this agent is lurking around you, know that this too shall pass. Know that you will be okay. You may need to change your life, a little or a lot. But change it in a way that you will be able to appreciate and live through. This is because you know how to live and enjoy life, or you are willing to learn. You know more today than you did yesterday or years ago. Take those lessons and start a new life with good memories and learned lessons.

NOTE: All reported suicides are not the result of diagnosed emotional, mental or mind conditions. They are reported as this being the cause of death, but these incidents could be made to look like intentional suicides and are instead homicides that often are uninvestigated. These suicides could also be caused by side effects of medications or drugs that can cause immediate chemical changes in the body, thus resulting in a harmful action. These incidents can arise with no pre-existing emotional, mental or mind condition or with people who are diagnosed with a condition but managing it well. Therefore, this would not be their choice.

Think about some of the reported suicides in the media. Happy, successful people, in the middle of doing what they love and then they are gone. Reported as self-induced or self-inflicted injuries. These causes are accepted with no investigation or questions asked. So, what if they have been diagnosed and undergoing treatment. If they wanted to end their lives, they would not be seeking help to live better, happier, and longer lives by taking treatments. Let's think about what can be done to bring clarity to these incidents.

The first step is to stop being afraid to talk about suicide and mind/mental health, as if talking about it will invite it to visit. Second is to understand the different reasons and ways that people choose to end their lives, as they know it, and finally to help guide individuals of all ages to living a healthy, happy and self-loving life, first and foremost.

What this agent does not want you to know, are the options available to you. Options that you can change your life one step at a time. Options that making life changing decisions is easier than you think. Options that life could be better, if given a chance.

Question: Is it possible that you can be under the care of professionals and this urge appears or becomes stronger? The answer is yes, because this agent can be the result of bad health, bad direction, chemical imbalances, medications, mind control and mind manipulation. These all can be introduced by anyone near or far, even if you are under the care of a professional. Stay strong aware and awake. This makes you powerful.

When you make the decision to seek professional help, get a referral from someone that you know and trust. Get this referral and start speaking to them even before feeling down and ready for a change. This is when your mind is in a better place. When you are happy and can research and begin the process of keeping a clear mind and this thing out of your way. Seeking professional help? Some people prefer Psychologists, where no medicine is prescribed, while they seek find the root of the problem. Some seek Psychiatrists, who are also medical doctors and who can prescribe medicine for the soul, which may be needed for the body to get settled. Medicines could have side effects which can cause sadness, depression, and suicidal thoughts.

So just be mindful and ask the important questions about your care plan. Both Professionals will schedule follow-up appointments to track the progress of their clients. Investigate and compare the two professions and make the best choice for you. When choosing to speak with professionals, ask if you can record your sessions. If they say no, then you may want to find someone else to use. Request that they speak with family members, friends, and co-workers in recorded sessions, so that you can listen back on those conversations as well.

Sometimes we are so involved in the doings of this and that for others, that we are removed from our own lives. Or we are so preoccupied with life's issues that often outsiders, our family, and friends, can see in us and around us what we miss. Therefore, speaking with others who know us can be helpful. Imagine feeling blue, feeling down, in need of help and you go to seek help, and then the help tells you that there is no need to speak with anyone else in your circle. They tell you that your words, your version is good enough. HUH? Sometimes those in your circle may have more details to fill in the blanks.

Please know that our story is always going to be our story,

which is why we are looking for help. The question then is, "how accurate is our story?" Should someone else close to you verify what is happening in your life? Just to make sure all is correct in what you are sharing. Maybe speaking with a spiritual non-denominational Chaplain will help. Non-denominational, because if we belong to and have been faithfully attending religious services, we have been guided by this faith, and we may need a different angle to help us find our way back to a happier life. Not converting just having guidance to help get you back on track.

Grab some paper, a pen, or a keyboard to write down your thoughts or even a recorder to speak your thoughts. This is something that can be done using your cell phone device. Whichever method or methods you choose, listen to, or read what has come from you. It is especially important to hear your story through your own ears. So read it aloud, or have it read to you. It will resonate differently in your mind, coming from the outside in.

When you are regularly thinking of something repeatedly in your mind with the same abilities that you have, you will get the same results. When you write it and read it, or record it and listen back, those same thoughts will enter a different area of your brain. It then processes in that area giving you a different perspective, coming from a different angle or way. Try it.

The profile of suicide and mind/mental health conditions are discussed in this chapter. Some of the accessories and other things that can lead to ending the life that you know will be discussed later. This is not a how to end your life by way of suicide book. This is an awareness guide on how it can happen without you realizing that it is waiting patiently, and how we can stop it from winning. How we can change life, thereby ending the life that we know and creating a new one.

Good mind/mental health is so important and as you have read, there are many factors that can contribute to the wellness of the mind, our mood and how our decisions are made.

Watch the movie "Brain On Fire", true story and "13 Reasons Why", based on true events. Visit: BeatCancer.org for Cancer Coaches and support, if there is a cancer illness that you or someone that you know is dealing with.

Please read on…

Mind Is Too Mental As Teeth Are Too Dental

Notes

Mind Is Too Mental As Teeth Are Too Dental

Notes

Mind Is Too Mental As Teeth Are Too Dental

Notes

Chapter 2

We All Have A Mind

We all can be negatively challenged with mind/mental health conditions. I will call it, the "agent". People of all ages. Young children and adolescents are among the rising numbers. If you research this you will find that there is no specific race, age, gender, or profession that this agent will not target. It obviously has a passport because it strikes worldwide.

Professionals in all fields including Healthcare Workers, EMT's, Paramedics, Doctors, Nurses, Dentists are very high in numbers. Flight Attendants, Pilots, Law Enforcement Officers, Teachers, Bankers, and Military members are among a growing number of victims. Teenagers and others who live in low sunlight areas due to vitamin D deficiency, suffer with sadness, depression, and suicides. This D deficiency could also be the cause of many health conditions like arthritis, immune system disorders, weak bones, seasonal deficit disorder, diabetes, obesity, cancer, nerve disorders and muscle conditions. These conditions can happen to people who are living in any area of the world, and especially if they aren't getting enough sunlight.

This could also be the reason why home daycare providers, and other people who spend a lot of time in the house, are being diagnosed with cancer and other conditions, because they are not getting enough sunlight or vitamin D. The body is deficient of vitamin D, and conditions can arise. If this is how you feel, check your D levels, take a quality vitamin D supplement and or eat D rich foods year-round. Vitamin D is actually a hormone, and very useful in many areas of our bodies. Don't worry just get some sun and be happy!

Inner city communities and young people around the age of thirteen are victims of sadness, depression, and suicidal thoughts, more often than we know. There is a history of suicides with college students as well. The numbers are high and blamed on academic pressures and other factors. Are there other sources that may be influencing these conditions amongst students of all ages? More recently children, pre-teens and teens are suffering with these conditions at high rates. These situations are even blamed on the internet, bullying and peer pressures. But could it be something else contributing to the cause?

As we now know, pharmaceuticals can cause chemical changes in the body that can give people these thoughts and feelings. Is it worth further research to see if there is a relationship with age-related, scheduled, or seasonal recommended medications for children, adolescents, and adults, that can lead to these actions? These scheduled events may cause protein deficiencies that could create chemical imbalances, leading to these thoughts and actions or other mind/mental health conditions.

Protein deficiencies can cause sadness, mood changes, depression, and suicidal thoughts. Are these routine medications causing protein deficiencies and mind/mental health issues in the body? Maybe? Therefore, keeping your protein levels up with food and supplements, like whey protein, protein bars, drinks, peanuts, beans, meats that are lean but high in protein, can keep your mind/mental health in a great place. Check the internet for high protein foods and be creative.

Mind Is Too Mental As Teeth Are Too Dental

Certain medications can cause a person to feel a way, that can change their life and the lives of many. We see, read, and hear, "can cause suicidal thoughts" warnings when medications, created in laboratories, are advertised. However, no one says why or how or even what those thoughts would sound like. It is said that there is a direct relationship in the number of chromosomes in some people, which may cause mind/mental health conditions to be present.

Odd that a popular laboratory that makes baby formula was successfully sued, class action, for genetic testing over 30 years ago. What are the results of what they did? What effect is it having on children long term, some who are now adults? Oh, and yes, they are still in the baby formula business as of today. Knowing how these chemicals can affect the wellbeing and development of babies, children, adolescents then adults, you would think that there would be more oversight.

Young people, please know that your peer pressures will pass. Stay strong. Your beauty, looks and physical appearance is who and why you are you. No competition involved. These things may change as you continue to grow and develop, but in the meantime, be the best you, that's possible. Stay strong.

Your grades will change, improve with more concentrated effort, or learning from another source like the internet for independent study. All things can change as we continue to develop.

There is no need for you to be intimidated by others, especially those who are not feeding you, keeping a roof over your head and clothing you. If pressures are coming from outside or from the adults in your life, ask for a conversation or write a note to express how these pressures are affecting you. Find a solution together.

Parents, the concerns and some of the pressures that are put on children to succeed should be transferred into understanding how they learn. Find out what plans they have for their futures. Understanding why they are not able to succeed in some areas of life and then providing the correct resources to help them improve. This may be a better approach. We all learn differently. Patience is best when used to understand, not command.

This agent lurks deep within so many people without them knowing it. There are also many accessories that can lead to people having mind/mental health conditions and ending their lives by death. Some have past experiences that are hardly remembered but are reflected in the way that they live. Some of these experiences are from infancy and some throughout their lives. These are experiences that can lead to self-destructive behaviors, which can allow these agents to enter, find a place and to grow.

We overlook so many situations that we are confronted with daily. We get upset, argue, drink, overeat, smoke, and take risky actions during our lives. We have physical health conditions that can get us down and feeling bad, without ever realizing that, from these situations, deposits are being made in the soil of the soul, in which this agent could be growing. We are feeding it without knowing that it is there.

"Talk to someone." That is what is advised when someone is dealing with depression, sadness, emotional illness, mental illness, drug abuse and other addictions. But again, who do you talk to about these incidents when they are happening? Is it a Friend, a Teacher, a Social Worker, a Clergy Member, a Psychologist, or a Psychiatrist? Remember, who we talk to, will have a great impact on the results that we will get. Everyone who appears to be a friend, may not be. Everyone who wears the professional hat, is not necessarily fit for the position. We all have history, and we bring that history into how we make decisions in our chosen professional lives. So don't be afraid to ask questions of those who you choose to speak with.

Getting referrals is important from those who you trust. Use the referral as a preventive tool, in advance of needing it, so as not to need it in an emergency. An ounce of prevention is worth more than a pound of cure. Remember we all have a mind, so we all have mind/mental health conditions, great, good, not so good or in need of assistance. So, speaking to someone about you and life is okay and good, no matter your mind/mental condition, you may motivate the listener, who may be able to share that information with someone else.

The question is, when you do get to speak to someone, where do you start? Is it from early childhood where sometimes bullying and abuse begins? Like on the playground, in school, or at home where some parents were their first bully experience? Or do you begin at adolescence, where a semi-freedom began, and choices start being introduced as exciting dares and the "prove you are grown" challenges start arriving from your peers?

Mind Is Too Mental As Teeth Are Too Dental

Here is an example of where we can improve as adults. We say "don't do drugs" but we hardly explain what the drugs would look like, and who and how they may be introduced. For example, "Oh take this it will help you sleep or relax or study harder." We also don't show how they would look, even those drugs that are available "over the counter." Use your device to show an idea of how these drugs can look, from pills, to powders, to laced marijuana, and including alcohol drinks.

Many young people have succumbed to death by mixing energy drinks, over the counter medications and other items. Could these mixes and health conditions have a fatal outcome? Sure, if we don't know the inner health conditions of our own bodies. We need to have more complete physical examinations at the medical office visits. Visit the "Nutrition and Wellness" page on my website NetworkingForSuccess.info to access the "Adding Your 2 Cents" Health and Wellness Examination Form.

Research and save the information about the chemicals in all the products that you use, in one day. We should have a more in depth understanding of the products we use and how they affect the condition of our bodies. This is before an illness sets in. This will be to prevent illnesses of all types. We need to have clearer conversations about offers and choices. This includes questioning professionals who offer or prescribe medications. We need to weigh the possible risks, versus the possible benefits and seek other options, in some cases, for better outcomes.

So, back to the talk, where do you begin this talk? Maybe the starting point is, as an adult in an abusive relationship, or job intimidation. Where do we begin if we cannot remember where it started? Start from as early as you can remember and work your way forward. The process will be cleansing and may reveal more than we know. By the time we get to the real issue, we should feel more comfortable talking about our current life situations. Whether, to yourself on a recording device or to someone else, just start talking. That is the goal, right?

Now here you are a teenager or an adult with this agent in your midst. It is imbedded deeply, ready and waiting to attack. This sneaky sneak is offering an option that appears to be the answer to all the problems that are in your life right now. This sneaky sneak preys on the strong when they are at a point of weakness. Loss of loved ones, loss of income, loss of all hope and here it comes to the "rescue". This is not the rescue. This is not the answer.

Mind Is Too Mental As Teeth Are Too Dental

Stay Awake. Stay Aware. This agent, suicide, is not the answer. It is not the answer. This agent is the weaker of all, because at your strongest it knows that it faces serious challenges. It may not win at that time. It will usually show up if there is an instance of weakness in your life. From anything that is discussed here, or whatever else can weaken you temporarily. Not necessarily due to anything that you have done or asked for, just other things in life that may happen.

Then again, as we know, there are the victims of the side effects of prescription drugs, causing changes in the body, that can bring sadness, depression, homicidal and suicidal thoughts to the forefront. The ones we know about, that are advertised and then there are those medications that do not advertise their lists of possible side effects. What about the combinations of these medications? What are the internal effects on the persons mind, and body who may be taking not just one medication, but several medications at one time or in the same day.

Are there studies on the interactions of these different drugs with each other? And the chemical make-up of these drugs? Whom do you ask? Do your research. Ask your Doctor at the time the medications are prescribed. Ask the Pharmacist when you have the prescriptions filled. The conflict of medications, alcohol and street drugs within the body can cause more harm than good. Question your parents or caregivers about your health history. Your falls and scrapes, stitches, and surgeries, wounds, though healed. Some of these things, you may not remember, or you may be unaware of. Check your medical history from childhood to now.

Do you know your blood type and the conflicts against better health, based on your blood type? Do you know the best foods you should be eating, for better health, based on your blood type. Did you know that this was important to know?

Research and learn about the importance of amino acids, which are needed in our bodies, to be healthy. Bananas have tryptophan which creates serotonin. Serotonin keep us in a good mood and our senses calm and happy. Bananas are also great to help regulate your blood pressure and they are a low glycemic (enters the blood stream slowly) sweet, which helps with blood sugar and natural energy. Just saying…

Have a bunch, one at a time, throughout the week.

Protein deficiencies in the body can be caused by several things like poor nutrition, or food content, chemical imbalances, chemical absorption, and medications. When this happens,

Mind Is Too Mental As Teeth Are Too Dental

your neurotransmitters are affected, thereby creating signal miscommunications. This can result in changes in our mood, it can also cause overeating, twitching, unexplained pain, memory loss, sadness, depression, suicidal and homicidal thoughts, just to name a few. Keep high protein foods in your diet, to remain in a good mind/mental state of being.

Suicidal thoughts have different ways of coming to you. Giving up due to medical conditions, influencing something that you are doing, in your normal routine, or just the thought of, what if…and how would someone react, if you ended your life. These thoughts and feelings can arrive in a very sneaky way.

True story: On a beautiful Saturday afternoon, a Lady was driving her car when she heard in her head this thought; "FASTER, FASTER, FASTER….NOW CRASH." Each faster getting louder. She stopped the car immediately. When she thought about what could have caused that to happen, she remembered a new medication she was given as a dialysis patient. She went home and read about it and one of the listed side effects was, "can cause suicidal thoughts." Think about that.

So casually injected, while she was doing something that she could do it with. Thankfully, she is a woman who was in her right mind at the time, and strong. She knew right from wrong. She is a person who was not struggling with life's issues, to the point where this thought would seem like a good idea. She knew that idea, was a wrong one, and not hers, because she was strong. Of course, she did not follow it. This is her story, and I am glad that it was shared with me, to share with you.

I hope that her lesson, her story will benefit others. But keep in mind, had she followed it, others would have told her story. "Aah she must have been tired, on dialysis for so long…yeah so sad…." They would have been telling a "lie" on her. She is not tired, she is not ready to leave, and thankfully she did not listen to those thoughts. So, she told her own story, as a survivor of the side effect and a winner over those thoughts. But keep in mind, most importantly, of how casual it could come in, chat and slide someone into causing an action, that would lead to such a devasting end. Sneaky and knowing….

No one talks about how it could sound. Not everyone who hears those similar thoughts may be in a good mind place. They could have life's issues coming down on them, like bills and financial troubles, bullying, relationship troubles, or an illness that is wearing them down. If that thought came, they may just listen and follow through because it would seem like the answer, to what may be troubling them. Suicidal thoughts? Hmmm…Who would think the thoughts could be so easily accessible and suggestive, while you are doing something that you can do it with. This is how, with no pre-existing mental/mind health issues, it can ease its way in, to casually suggest the idea of doing it, and someone could follow.

No signs, no missed conversations or behaviors, no note, or it can even engage you to write a note, expressing your thoughts and ideas of life, but still with no intentional reason at all to end it, just expressing life and feelings. A quick chemical imbalance, and a quick action at that time, is how this sneaky sneak can attack a healthy happy person and win. What an interesting conversation.

Donn't we see, hear, and read about this possibility in the commercials that are advertising medications? Without the explanation of how this could happen and what those thoughts would sound like. Someone sharing with us how to prevent these thoughts, would help. But what we get instead is the statement, "can cause sadness, depression and suicidal thoughts." The other thing we get is, "call your doctor." We should be speaking about what these "intrusive thoughts," as they are now called, by the young people, would say. What do they sound like? When does it happen? From survivors, ask the question, what were you thinking? Why did you attempt it? Ask the questions that we need the answers to. This is so we can better understand the actions that followed and to allow them to speak about the incident. Communication is the key to understanding most all things in life.

Mind/mental health conditions come so gradually, that the person or those around them don't notice anything different, until there is a major incident, followed by a diagnosis. This is a time where some people would try to hide the hurt, pain, and confusion. Alzheimer's and Dementia was "senile" back in the 1970's, my how things have changed.

Then there are the conditions that are immediate, no pre-existing signs. The person is normal and okay to the outside world. Go to work, come home, play with the children, cook dinner, go out with friends. Everything is normal, doing their homework, locked in the bedroom, (as always), go out with no destination stated. Normal everyday life. How was your day? Fine. Anything new? No. Okay, love you. Love you. As Always…so natural. Then suddenly…an outburst, a violent action, a result of some immediate chemical change in the body, that caused a neuro misfire, and the sirens are blaring.

So here is another accessory story. This gentleman a retired EMT (Emergency Medical Technician) was in the hospital as a patient. The nurses gave him his medications and he started feeling funny and asked them, "hey, what did you give me"? They just looked at him, ignored him and continued talking to each other. He became angry and louder and asked the same question again.

They look at him laughing and casually asked, "why, is it giving you suicidal thoughts?" He yelled NO! To his surprise the medications were giving him homicidal thoughts, telling him to pick up the scissors and stab the nurses in their necks. That descriptive. When he told them that, they were very shocked and immediately called the doctor. Hmmm.

As he told me this story, he was still very upset at the effect of the medications and the reactions of the nurses who seem to have felt, the suicidal thoughts were normal and acceptable. Again, he is a retired Emergency Medical Technician with experience in medically assisting people in crisis. That situation was a CRISIS! When you can get homicidal thoughts and actions that appear to be yours but are in fact, a result of chemical reactions in the body. Reactions that can cause such disturbing results, as murder and suicide, yes, that is a CRISIS.

Do you recall hearing such stories that may have been caused by these or similar reactions? For me, after hearing about the homicidal thoughts in his story, it made me think of the murder suicides reported in the news.

Imagine how someone would feel after blacking out due to an unknown chemical reaction, committing such a horrendous act, and when they return to normal and see what has been done, to their family members, friends, or co-workers, that scene alone could lead to the suicide action. In this case suicide wasn't the initial thought or plan, though it was the end action after seeing what had been done by them.

People focus on the "suicide" and begin to wonder and ask, why did the person have to kill others? When in fact it may have been because they killed the others, they then killed themselves. Many lives lost. Many lives affected. Many questions unanswered, until now. I hope.

When full disclosure is given to the public about the chemical

Mind Is Too Mental As Teeth Are Too Dental

ingredients in household cleaning products, prescriptions, cosmetics, and their possible side effects, people will begin to make better choices on what they will use and how. We may then stop hearing, reading, and experiencing these drastic results. Some of these ingredients can also be in street drugs and social alcohol products. Hmmm… Never know.

This may explain occurrences happening around the world, affecting a multitude of lives forever, with so much destruction at hand. We make assumptions, and questions are asked as to why people behave in such erratic and harmful ways to each other. With very few real answers found, until now.

Other victims of this agent are greater in numbers. They are the loved ones of those who have passed on from suicidal actions. We call them Victims of Loves Lost. They are the loved ones left to wonder why and left with so many unanswered questions. How could this happen to such a nice person? Why didn't they see it coming? Why didn't the victim talk to them about how they must have been feeling?

But we now know those questions can have very different answers, including, there was nothing to talk about, there were no pre-existing conditions. In some cases, they didn't know where to begin the conversation. So, start talking and listening with interest in the talk, even with yourself, written or verbally recorded on your device.

Be a good listener. (t)

Then we have the survivors who attempted suicide and thankfully failed, and those thinking about it. Talk to someone who attempted this act and was unsuccessful. Don't be afraid of the subject. Don't be afraid to talk about it. Don't be ashamed to talk about it, if you are the survivor. Be thankful for life again with knowledge and more power.

Communication is the key to understanding. Silence could be the fuel that may re-ignite this flame again. Yes, a survivor will probably be involved in therapy however, the angles from where these thoughts arrived, may not be fully addressed in therapy.

Therapy will most likely come from a clinical perspective and maybe after medications have been administered. Which in fact, the medications may not have been necessary. They usually become the first line of treatment, with the assumption that the survivor was having emotional, mental/mind issues that led to this attempt. The attempt may have been a quick chemical imbalance, an unexplainable, unintentional, unknowing act. Remember, a chemical imbalance can cause a happy person to perform this act. Clinically, a complete blood screening, an EEG (electrical brain scan) and a CAT scan of the brain should be conducted, and the results reviewed by various departments in the hospital before administering psychotic medications.

Why? Because the results of these tests may show something going on in the body, physically, but not in the mind totally, or not an emotional condition.

People come into the emergency room with behaviors defined as mental illnesses, they are given psychotic drugs that are used to change the chemical structure in the mind. This treatment may cause more harm, before possible good, if good at all.

However, keep in mind that those screening tests may find that the source of this behavior may have been a reaction to chemical changes in the body, accidental overdose of prescriptions, if they forgot they took them, street drugs or alcohol poisoning. Once they start receiving psychotic drugs, then here we go again. More reactions, diagnosis, and misdiagnosis, creating a problem with someone who was happy and healthy before this occurrence, and not in need of these drugs.

This person may have needed these tests and complete blood, and urine screening including protein levels, a detoxed, rehydration and rest. Then a talk after the rest. Hospital Administrators should create a team that's trained to review all angles when a survivor is presented at the hospital. This is especially important whether there is prior history of mental/mind illness or not, or if the staff is unsure of the history. Ask for this protocol if you are with a person who attempted this act.

Find out what is really going on with them, that made them act in such a way. Ask them what made them feel like this is what they wanted to do. When they tell you they don't know, you may want to believe them. They may not know, and they may not know what you are talking about. They may ask you where they are, what happened and why are they in the hospital.

When they tell you they heard voices in their head, ask them to tell you what the voices said. Don't be afraid to talk this out and through, with the person. It is not contagious, but it can be continuous, if we do not talk about it. It's not the boogie man

Mind Is Too Mental As Teeth Are Too Dental

or maybe it is. Fear is the fact that all things are possible, so think positive and move into a better understanding for a better life. If this has happened to someone close to you, ask for a forensic autopsy to check all levels of chemicals in the body. Insurance companies will not pay off on suicides within the first 2 years.

However, we are learning that all reported suicides are not, and some are not the intention of the victim. So, despite what "they" say is the cause of death, request a forensic autopsy paid with the insurance policy, and billed through the funeral home. It's best to be rest assured of the cause of a loved one's death, by any means. Even if there was a note.

Well, the survivors and victims of loves lost are present today to help stop this sneaky sneak in its tracks. To be victorious in this movement. To get relief from the mystery and possible feelings of guilt, for not knowing what to do, or what could have been done to prevent this from happening. Relief from not knowing what you did or didn't see or hear. We are here to end the trail of unnecessary actions that would lead to death, We are here with a weapon called "communication."

Let's talk about it and move it out of the way as fast as we can!

Suicide is a serious act, let's end it today, and all its causes as well. Keep a full understanding of the different mind/mental health conditions that can be caused by chemical imbalances, that may be treated with natural supplements. Like L-theanine for anxiety, which can also be caused by low iron, and the relationship of Dopamine levels associated with Parkinson's and Schizophrenia, too little and too much. Let's talk about it all.

Mind Is Too Mental As Teeth Are Too Dental

Contact the National Suicide and Crisis Lifeline

Text or Dial 988

Veterans and Active Military Preventing Substance Abuse and Suicide: https://www.linesforlife.org/mhl/ or

Text 838255

The deaf and hard of hearing can contact the Lifeline via TTY.

Dial 711

http://www.suicidepreventionlifeline.org/ GetHelp/LifelineChat.aspx

Suicide Prevention Resource Guide

http://www.sprc.org/resources-programs/program-encourageactive-rewarding-lives-pearls

Association of Black Psychologists

http://www.abpsi.org/find-psychologists

Association of Psychiatry

www.Psychiatry.org

Mind Is Too Mental As Teeth Are Too Dental

Notes

Mind Is Too Mental As Teeth Are Too Dental

Notes

Mind Is Too Mental As Teeth Are Too Dental

Notes

Mind Is Too Mental As Teeth Are Too Dental

There are victims on all sides of this act of suicide.

he survivors who need our love, understanding and talks.

The victims of loves lost, like family, and friends and those who continue to question themselves, wondering what they could have done to prevent this.

The professionals who cared for and about the loved one, also feel a great sense of loss on a human and personal level.

Many times, the love and time together was enough to keep that person strong, for as long as they were able to stay strong.

You did all you could do, with what you knew.

Talk to the survivors and see what they need to live a healthy and happy life.

It is sometimes bigger than us, but we should always strive to purposefully be our best, that is what may matter the most.

No Regrets, No Guilt, Just Memories, and Gratefulness to Have Known that Loved One and Enjoyed Your Time Together!

Keep Living!

Chapter 3

The Traps

Diagnosis of different illnesses; physical mental or emotional may have caused this agent to grow like a giant in some people, almost instantly. People get the doomsday diagnosis, "Nothing else we can do for you.". Well, if not you then who? That is what you should ask them. You should also ask "Then exactly what were you doing all along with the treatments and ongoing management of my condition?"

Second and third opinions are important before moving to treatment options*. So now that we know a little more, we should ask questions first. Ask about your options ahead of time. Whatever you do, just do not give up. Get ready to fight for your life. Realize those spoken words are from one source.

Mind Is Too Mental As Teeth Are Too Dental

Get your diagnosis, prognosis, treatment plan and expected timeline for results in writing, so you can read it, over and over and track your progress. Also start recording your visits with your Doctor. These medical conversations are sometimes a bit complicated and moving fast with a lot of information being shared. You may not be able to remember everything. So, announce and record. Or just start recording for your better understanding.

Once you understand the condition, find other sources of treatment, and compare, like Chinese medicine or Naturopathic resources and Practitioners through InviteHealth.com as an example. Pick up a copy of the "Back to Eden" book*** and Where There Is No Doctor. You should seek these sources now before you are sick, so that you may not get sick. Shop at stores that support the information in these books. I recommend Invite Health and Remedies Herb Shop*** with online availability. Seek and ye shall find.

The diagnoses that people get are defined by who? What has caused these conditions? Most people who are diagnosed with chronic depression, are told that they are depressed based on symptoms described in a book, or on television and radio commercials. You are sick from an unknown cause, they don't know the root of the problem just the symptoms. You get treatment for the symptoms and you still you don't know the root cause. Now have new symptoms different from the first ones. Why is that? What is the effect of these treatments when the cause is still present and unknown?

Finding the root sources of the symptoms that you are experiencing, should be the start to the treatment process for any ailment. When you treat the symptoms and not know the root causes, the body can become confused. Internal chemical changes to whatever is going into the body can cause thoughts of ending life. Yours or someone else's, as we have learned.

Ok maybe I feel sad, lonely and with no way out, but "why", is the real question and for how long? When did you or anyone in your circle first notice these changes? These are particularly important questions that should be asked, and the answers found to get to the root of the problem. Communication.

The "inflammation" auto immune diseases, like the cancer family, multiple sclerosis, diabetes, multiple myeloma, the fibrosis family, lupus, eczema, sarcoidosis, scleroderma; what has caused all these illnesses? You were not born this way so what has changed? Is it your diet your environment, your home, or your workplace? Is it in the air that you are breathing, the water that you drink, or bathe in, sprayed perfumes, make-up, colognes, deodorants, your household cleaning products, your hair products, and of course the foods you are eating?

Your home you ask? Well, yes. If you have foundation cracks in your walls or in the basement, radon gas can seep through and cause illnesses including cancer. This is possible in your home or your workplace. Especially if you work from home and spend a lot of time there. Check it out and have it checked. Then your household cleaning products. Many of the chemicals can seep into your sinuses, then your brain and into your bloodstream through your skin. Did you know the skin is the bodies largest organ? It's an opening into your bloodstream as well.

Your heating system can cause sickness including cancer. Black soot, poor ventilation, clogged exhaust systems, all of these can allow bacteria, viruses, cancer causing elements into your living space. You will breathe these things in. Babies will crawl in these sediments. Family members can become ill, with constant respiratory infections, as well as have symptoms of unknown causes. Sounds familiar? Can these things affect your mood and thinking? Well, yes, they can.

True story: In my home I noticed an unexplained amount of dust even after cleaning. I looked around to find the source. I figured it came from the heat vent. I taped a large white air conditioning filter over the vent for six hours. When I removed it, the filter was pitch black, after only six hours later.

You know that I changed it and covered it for the rest of my lease. Yes, of course I informed the landlord and other tenants in the house as well.

Check your heating and air conditioning systems (HVAC Heating Ventilation and Air Conditioning). The vents and filters should be cleaned and or changed periodically, at home and at your workplace. You cannot change these things at work, but you can alert maintenance or your supervisor of the condition if you see the problem is there.

What chemicals are in household cleaning products and how safe are they to use? How safe are perfumes and other cosmetics? This may sound strange, but some of the chemicals used, and combined with others to create these products, are extremely dangerous to humans. This information is out there for you to see. Take a minute or two with your technology device, to research the ingredients of the products that you use that touch your skin. Find out the level of protective garments used by the workers in the labs and factories that create them. Use your device.

The hospitals will never, test you for these chemicals as the cause of your illness. If you work in any of those labs or factories and exposure occurs, the area hospitals will have specific procedures to test and treat you for exposure. But guess what? You are exposed every time you use these products.

Do you recall a questionnaire form at your doctors' office asking about these common items that are mentioned here? Do you feel these are important questions that should be asked at the medical offices? Cosmetics, detergents, perfumes, colognes, deodorants, lotions? All full of chemicals. Do you feel these things listed and the combination of chemicals that create them could affect your health and mind condition?

Visit our website and get a copy of the "Adding Your 2 Cents" Health and Wellness Examination Form. In the meantime, research the regular products that you use, and how those chemicals can affect your body.

Mind Is Too Mental As Teeth Are Too Dental

True Story: There was a Lady who was sick all the time. Diagnosed with an auto immune disease and she could not get better. Her daughter asked her to stop using her cosmetics, including her perfume, make-up, and hair care products. After about a month, she noticed a change in her health. After a longer time without the use of those products, she got even healthier.

You see, without a degree in medicine, her daughter was able to use "observation and deductive reasoning" to improve her Moms health. The simple things that can make you or break you and improve your health and wellness are at your fingertips.

Prescriptions are given to some people who receive a diagnosis of depression, with one of the side effects listed as, "can cause suicidal thoughts." To that we say, "Really, well thanks a lot." The influences that can cause mind/mental health conditions and actions, can start in so many ways, even from illnesses.

The illness or the treatment can cause sadness and depression, which was not the condition from the beginning. The loss of loved ones can create no desire to do anything social, and thoughts of suicide can come from being alone. When these occurrences happen, they may be treated with medications to help you, however, it can cause these feelings as well.

Medicine has a purpose. Immediate and urgent, to get control of the issue. Medicine is not necessarily for long term management, but you won't know, unless you take the time to figure out the why. It's so important Your condition may not be your fault. Take your time and find the "Why"!

Other traps to consider would be street drugs and alcohol use. Both of which can alter your thinking and your decisions. They can make you see things that are not there. Hear people that are not present. Spin around in the street. Sleep all day and up all night. These elements can cause you to feel like the world is ending. It just may be, however, you will not remember it, if it happens. Just be mindful of these reactions when choosing your pleasure.

Think about that. These uses can cause you to make decisions that affect you and your family's safety. They can take you away from here mentally, and when you are back here, with us, you will ask "Wow...what happened? Thankfully you made it back. Some people do not escape these traps so easily and they do not make it back to this side with their loved ones.

SSI Disability: There are people who claim illnesses to receive SSI payments which is making life financially comfortable for them. Guess what, if you are not sick, you will get sick from the treatments administered for your fake condition. Before you know it, you may have these agents growing wild in your body, caused by the side effects of the medications and misguidance, based on the story you are telling.

Your body can become a big ball of lethal confusion, from unnecessary treatments. This can now lead to required medications and treatments based on the way you are responding.

Lyrics in music can stimulate the growth of bad mind/mental thoughts. Certain songs can promote and welcome this agent into the minds of some people who are listening. Vicious and message filled programs watched on all forms of media, offer subliminal thoughts and suggestions into the minds and hearts of those watching. If these are bad messages, then bad thoughts may come from them. There again, is when an opening of the door may happen. This can allow it to sneak in, wait or attack. Even when times are good, it finds a way in because it is all around and at all ages.

Mind Is Too Mental As Teeth Are Too Dental

STOP, STOP, STOP, listening to and reading negative "its normal" material. Because it is sold, do not mean it is gold. The term "food for thought" is so powerful when you think about it. It is what we eat, read, listen to, and watch, because when everything goes into the brain there it stays. What goes in will have some type of an effect on your thinking, your dreams, and your everyday living. It is designed for that purpose.

Know that because it is funny does not make it good. Because it is approved, do not make it safe, for everyone.

People who follow the news, hear, or read about death, destruction, rape, murder and then wonder why their day didn't go so well, are not paying close attention to what they are attracting. They wonder why they don't rest well at night. Reflect on your actual intake of everything, including caffeine late in the day. Just saying.

The traps allow this agent to sneak in and grow, and the traps are all around us. But remember this agent is weak, and it will have to fight harder to win when you are at your strongest. SO, STAY STRONG!

*Side Notes: Insurance companies have policies that pay you for covered illnesses and accidents. What you do with that money is up to you. Your second and third opinions may not be covered by your health insurance company, because they want to save money. You can use these payments to do what you want or need to once your claim is processed. Watch the Aflac video on my YouTube.com@evadynesmith3986 to learn more.

Also, to give you more strength and power, Whole Life Insurance can provide you with funds if diagnosed with a critical illness, and that can make a difference in your care. As well, Whole Life policies can provide financial relief for money troubles, that may not be allowing you to be happy. We can help with your insurance needs. Feel free to contact us.

Check out bio-curcumin (turmeric), fiv-loxin (frankincense), and ginger as anti-inflammatories to fight inflammation which is what causes most diseases in our bodies. Pure green tea, (do not mix with cow's milk) whole star anise, sour sop, aged garlic, bladder wrack as an anti-inflammatory, it has a positive effect with the treatment of certain cancers and for thyroid health, and sea moss both have a host of vitamins and minerals to help with better health.

Guinea root to kill cancer cells. Krill and SOD for better brain health. Alcar (Acetyl L-Carnitine) with ALA, amino acids, probiotics, prebiotic foods, cruciferous veggies (broccoli, cauliflower, cabbage, brussels sprouts, and asparagus) just check out the nutritional value of your green veggies and all the other vegetables, fruits and foods. To rid metal toxins and from your body, use kelp and pristine chlorella, they remove radiation and toxic metals including mercury from your body. Alcar (Acetyl L-Carnitine) helps to rebuild the coating that protects your nerves, which could provide neuropathy relief.

Great health starts with great nutrition. Check out the nutritional and medicinal benefits of "bananas". They have tryptophan which creates serotonin for a boost of energy and mind/mental/mood wellness. They help with other health benefits including, lowering your blood pressure and they are low glycemic which is good for diabetics.

Turmeric has nutritional and medicinal values for depression, inflammation, cancer fighting and circulation, and it stops bleeding from cuts, just pack it on and wait 20 minutes, brush off and re pack. You will begin to feel a whole lot better when you see clearer, the value of natural remedies and begin to use them. Burdock root is a great blood cleanser, anti-inflammatory and it helps with weight loss. The mushrooms family is a great source for wellness and the maitake mushroom helps reduce cancer cell reproduction.

**Visit the website www.NetworkingForSuccess.info and click on "Nutrition and Wellness" link, there you will find Invite Health to order great products and receive valuable information. Call them and speak to Nutritionist and Naturopathic Practitioners including Jerry Hickey Lead Scientific Officer, Pharmacist and Nutritionist. Many of the team members at Invite Health are knowledgeable about health, wellness, medicine, and nutrition. You may email Jerry your health questions to: JHickey@invitehealth.com He will respond. Listen to their podcasts on a variety of health subjects on their website. You can order from NFSPCN.com as well.

Check out BlackMagik363 on YouTube, Namaskar.com, QueenAfua.com, YahkiAwakened.com and they will lead you to others, on your journey to better health and wellness. For High Quality Dr. Lee Green Tea, go to Tea-For-Health.com/623

Check out the talk series "Evadynè with Company...Talk Worth Listening Too" on NetworkingForSuccess.info, Spotify, YouTube: @evadynesmith3986, and Huddle.Team Meeting ID Grownfolk The Talks offers information on life in general, relationships, cancer treatment and prevention, visit BeatCancer.org. We talk about health and wellness, mind/mental health, building wealth with life insurance, and so much more.

Watch the videos on YouTube with Dr. Ash, on Sick and Tired, Dr Gwen Scott, GwenScottND.com. For wellness consultation and Reiki services, contact Sister Nabihah through NabihahGarden.com or email: Nabihah.Sharrieff46@gmail. For great Vison Care information and direction, contact John Monroe: help@DrBanker.com visit: DrBanker.com For overall wellness listen to Abdul on YouTube.com@thehealthmanshow

Listen to Dr. Ray Omid speak on the value of Chiropractic Care on YouTube.com/@dr.rayomid7939 Hear his talks on the exceptional benefits that spinal re-alignment can have on improving the health and wellness conditions of the body. Once we understand how our body's central nervous system works, it may all make sense to us. High stage cancer and auto immune diseases can improve, with spinal adjustments.

When there is a lack of or no neurological fuel getting to the targeted areas of the body, that area will not function properly, including not at all. Therefore, this can cause illnesses to form and worsen. If you do not feed the source, it will die, then you may have a sore inside the body that can grow and grow wild. Your spine protects your nerves. When nerves are pinched, severed, or blocked, the nerves cannot fully communicate messages to the parts of the body they are assigned to. If this is fuel and food for that part of the body and it is not fed, yes it will cease to live. This could result in tumors, cancers, cysts, headaches, diabetes, limb debilitating disorders, hair loss and a host of other health conditions.

Pull up a human body diagram on your device and check out the nervous system. We are a very detailed, piece of art, and we deserve to fully understand our beauty firsthand. Watch videos on the internet to learn a little something every week.

*** Check out Remedies Herb Shop to fulfill your "Back To Eden" and "Where There Is No Doctor" book orders. https://remediesherbshop.com On my first visit, I spun around like Dorothy of Oz asking myself, "where can I get a resource guide for this store?" I knew it was a beautiful place, that totally resonated with my being. Then Back To Eden popped in my head, and Where There Is No Doctor. I had not seen either of these books in over a decade, but my clear head allowed for a flipping through the memory files, and there it was. If this is

Mind Is Too Mental As Teeth Are Too Dental

your cup of tea, Remedies Herb Shop will serve you well. There's no place like home and I have given you all that you need…here on Mother Earth.

If you want to quit smoking, I have an idea: It starts with Ginger Snap Cookies. You can choose a brand like Stauffer's Ginger Snaps; they are very strong with flavors and no high fructose corn syrup. Take a minute and break the cookies in four pieces. Each time you want to have a smoke, put one piece in your mouth and just let it sit on your tongue. Eventually eating it, but more importantly letting it dissolve on your tongue and taking in the flavors of the cookie. It should satisfy your desire for a smoke. You may need to start with a half cookie depending on your desire. Try it.

If you are afraid of weight gain when you quit, just start speeding up your metabolism especially before eating. They say high aerobic exercise early in the morning will speed up your metabolism and burn calories for up to 12 hours. Oh, and you may not be eating more, it's that nicotine also burns calories, so you had some help. Just dance and keep moving… Now why do I think the ginger snaps will? Well, I had a customer who said she wanted to quit smoking. I gave her my idea, using Nabisco ginger snaps. She yelled and asked, Why did you say that? I told her because I believe it will work, from the flavors. She asked again in a fearful way. I asked her if she prayed to God to help her stop smoking, she said yes. I said, then that's why I said it. In the end, she told me she loved ginger snap cookies, had not had any in over 20 years. The night before we met, she purchased 2 boxes thinking she would eat some that night, which didn't happen. She began to ask me about her sister's condition and advise on it. Funny but true...I referred her to Invite Health.

There is so much to learn about health and wellness to keep people in a good place. There are Doctors who are advising amino acids for the brain health and to help fight depression. Our bodies are the greatest machines ever created, it too needs to be tuned up, oiled, washed out and adjusted at times. We need to top off and replace nutrients and minerals, as our bodies may be unable to produce them naturally or have stopped due to our growing process.

We have a physical body that requires necessary elements as we grow up. Once we reach certain stages, our body naturally stops the production of some of these elements. Life, however, tends to break us down with the hard, unexpected tasks that we perform every day.

Mind Is Too Mental As Teeth Are Too Dental

Therefore, to run well, we must resupply the body with what it needs. The resupply of resources, to rebuild and strengthen our bodies will come from a healthy diet which may include vitamins and supplements. Preferably from natural organic food-based products. There are professionals and companies whose missions are really focused on helping the human body stay well. They are doing their best to share that information. Some were spoken about earlier. Look into Dr. Sebi, and LiveGood.com/Evadyne This is just to name a few.

There are many other Doctors and professionals who, with their knowledge of nature, who do all they can to encourage better health for all. Follow Dr. Oz, he steers you in the right direction. In the mid 1990's he co-wrote an important book titled "YOU" The Owner's Manual." You can find it on his website or mine.

Why do we need an owner's manual? Well don't you have an owner's manual for your refrigerator, television, telephone, and computer? What is it good for? Exactly! "YOU" is the guide to how we are designed and how we can stay operating well and live longer and healthier. It teaches us how to effectively operate our bodies and get the best use out of it. What a silly question. Why do we need an owner's manual? Lol

Dr. Oz is certified in both nutrition and medicine. The medical industry is not about nutrition, it is about medicine. Their course of study offers little or no mandatory studies in nutrition. They discredit nutrition and its' beneficial value to staying in a life of good health and wellness, however, utilizing nutrition as a key source of wellness, healing and preventing diseases, is always a natural way.

There is a Doctor who uses a special organic soup in his treatment with cancer patients. The organic ingredients include garlic, ginger, white potato peel, celery, cabbage, green onion, and cayenne pepper. Remember all organic ingredients. These items are antifungal foods, which helps to kill cancer cells. I would add burdock root, turmeric, bladder wrack and whole star anise for double power.

These items can be made as a juice as well. Research cancer fighting soup and eat well, to be well! A well-known cancer hospital uses burdock in their cancer treatment, look it up. Also, maitake mushrooms for cancer fighting properties. There is so much information online.

If you have questions about health conditions, use your technology device and ask the questions. You will get many answers. Ask for guidance from above, to guide you to the correct one or two, for you. Use your technology device to learn something new every day. If it is not going to hurt you, give it a try. Be mindful of who approves or disapproves care techniques. Be mindful that it is written "I have given you all that you need." Believe it. Many faith-based believers don't believe that natural resources are here to benefit us. Though they are believers.

We have available to us, all that we need to be whole, wise, and healthy, naturally. We need to know where to get it and how to use it. Seek and ye shall find. Hurry before all is lost from the forest fires that are destroying the natural resources that are here to protect the humans on Earth. Do your research on your device. You will learn a lot more.

Here is a partial list of diagnostic tests that can help with early detection and prevention of illnesses:

A1C for diabetes and glucose control detection

Amylase, Lipase and Fecal Elastase for pancreatic function

EEG for brain function (electroencephalogram)

CA-125 for ovarian cancer cell detection

Optical Coherence Tomography Macular Degeneration Eyes visit DrBanker.com for great eye exercises and information that can improve your vision.

Doppler Ultrasound for Arterial (blood flow and clots)

CRP levels of protein and inflammation markers

HS-CRP levels of heart focus protein and inflammation

PSA Prostate exam for Men

Microbiome Test for Gut health good and bad bacteria

Mammogram Breast Cancer Screening

Thermography test for inflammation in your body and can be used as a breast cancer screening test as well.

Chiropractic X-ray and Exam Misalignments of the spine

MRI and CAT Scan to check the addictive center in the brain for damage or under development which could explain all types of addictions also for the detection of many other conditions including migraines, cancer joint issues.

***Treatment and reversal of opioid addiction** in some countries, under medical supervision, with the use of the Iboga

Mind Is Too Mental As Teeth Are Too Dental

Plant*. It's a euphoric hallucinogenic plant that rewinds the mind from the addiction path and then rewinds your mind back to your natural path. This path is before the addiction and that's where it leaves you. Back home where you belong. Before the addiction. It's a monitored treatment process and said to be effective.

Look into Rythmia.com as another natural source to help you on your holistic journey to wellness.

*Contact us for insurance policies that pays you when a covered health event arises. You can use the money for anything that you wish including but not limited to second opinions, naturopathic treatments, household bills, wellness trips and much more. It is your money. The affordable policies include Disability, Hospitalization, Accident, Critical Illness, Cancer with Riders for Stroke, Sudden Cardiac Arrest, Heart Attack, End Stage Renal Failure, Initial Diagnosis and Recovery Benefits. We have life insurance with riders for long term care and critical illness conditions. Whole Life offers lump sum cash payments in the form of loans, to be used for any purpose you choose including financial crisis, and future financial plans for family members or yourself.

Contact us if you are looking for supplemental discount health plan memberships. These plans are becoming more popular and some offer shared costs and discounts on your services. Most importantly many of these membership plans will give You and your Doctor control of your healthcare decisions. These plans offer unique household options as well as family.

Watch the movie "Brain On Fire" a true story online, that shows just one case of how our brain works. It also shows the extent that diagnostics should go, to figure out the issue. Watch "13 Reasons Why" Season 1. It is based on real life events.

Watch: The Lake House, Bridges of Madison County, Reign On Me, Love on the Spectrum or any movie that makes you think and feel good.

I have another story to share about the brain and how it can work: A Young Lady named Carmen in her 90's heard a thump in another part of her house. She wondered what it was. It was her. She had fallen and hit her head. She didn't realize it at the time. It was like an outer body experience. She rose with 2 eggs on her forehead. She and I laughed as she told me this, and she asked that I add her story to this book. Where? I thought.

Mind Is Too Mental As Teeth Are Too Dental

But anywhere is great, as She is too.

We share Invite Health in common. Her condition could have been worse. Invites' products, her overall concern and consciousness of her health, her diet and of course her genes, all helped to keep her mind and body in great condition. Her mind, which is as sharp as ever and her bones strong, as she never broke anything with the many falls that she had. We attribute all her choices to her successful 90 plus year-old condition now. She has been a customer of Invite Health and the late Dr. Alan Pressman for over 50 years. Take a page from her book. Thank You to the entire Invite Health Team, for your guidance.

Why do I tell stories? It's how we learn. Because everything matters. Everyone has lessons and experiences that could shed light on other people lives. The stories can help put things into perspective, so that the reader or listener can visualize the best outcome. So, others can understand, it's not just them. It's not just me. It's not just You. We are all in it together, this life, of love, chance, happiness, loss, adventure, and sometimes disappointment. It's one story after another. Let's keep making stories, with adventure, love, joy, happiness and happiness.

Mind Is Too Mental As Teeth Are Too Dental

Notes

Mind Is Too Mental As Teeth Are Too Dental

Notes

Mind Is Too Mental As Teeth Are Too Dental

Notes

Mind Is Too Mental As Teeth Are Too Dental

Sickness; Disabilities; Social Conditions; Choice of Friends.

To see is one thing, to feel is something else.

But to listen and believe your body, is lifesaving!

When you hear something, feel your body and how it reacts.

How it reacts tells you if it is right or wrong.

Be a good listener!

Stay Up and Stay Aware!

Chapter 4

Botch Attempts

There are so many people who are ready to change their lives, end their lives in the same way that suicide and suicide attempts will do. I call these events "botched attempts." Here are some of the most common botched attempts.

You are sick and getting sicker and keeping it a secret. Keeping it "your personal business", that you do not want anyone to know about. This is because you do not want anyone to feel sorry for you. Well, you should feel sorry for yourself, because when you think about it, the only people who are aware of your condition are the medical staff. They are not around to help you through it at home. The thought of being alone should make you realize that you should share this with someone who loves

94

and cares about you.

Being alone through this process of dealing and healing can cause your condition to worsen. This is the time when you really need positive community support by your side. It also becomes a situation where your treatment providers are treating your symptoms and the possible oncoming conditions with what they know. Most, however, do not know the other sources that can support you emotionally, physically, and nutritionally.

Your support community, your family and friends may have information which can create a more holistic approach to your care. Medical Doctors know what they have been taught, but there is more to being and staying healthy than just medications. Some medical facilities are now incorporating nutrition into their care. Keep up on the natural ways of staying healthy, getting healthier and being of sound mind.

What do you do now? Do you keep it a secret, when at the same time you cannot spend quality time with family and friends? Now they start thinking that you are changing, lazy, angry, and other characteristics that carrying your secret alone can cause? If this continues, then guess what, you have a greater chance of becoming sad and lonely, and you will feel like the world is ending. This is because you did not tell anyone your secret before. Now you find it even harder to tell them. This can add stress to your healing and recovery. Support from positive, knowledgeable, and caring family members, friends and co-workers can uncover resources that may improve and even save your life. There are no secrets. So be the one to share your condition as soon as you know about it. Also getting a second opinion, so that your condition gets confirmed and does not worsen. Just tell them. Release it from your mind and be in a better place to heal.

Other botched attempts includes distractive living, driving, riding, or talking while under the influence. These are all very hazardous conditions. People who knowingly ride with people who are under an influence are taking a chance with their lives as well. Young people should not be drinking, however, if you are going to be out with friends select a designated driver who will be sober, not tired and having the ability to get you all home safely. It is the responsible thing to do.

Being in the way of any kind of traffic while walking, driving, or bike riding while you are operating a cell phone, including taking selfies is very dangerous to everyone involved. Being involved in accidents do not only affect the injured, but it also affects observers, family members and friends. Be mindful and keep focused. Think about the long-term results.

About drug and alcohol use or abuse. Some people are indulging to kill the pains they are having in life. Being under the influence allows them to forget, if only for a moment. The situation is the same when they are sober again. Some of these pains are emotional and some are physical. Whichever it is, let's hope people can find another way to face their issues, feel better, and learn to live happier with acceptance.

Then, there are those who are so tired that they can barely walk due to extreme exhaustion. Yes, they still make the decision to get behind the wheel to drive themselves and others. That normal quick blink of an eye can, take three seconds too many, to reopen and there goes an accident. Not only endangering the driver, but also putting others in harm's way. Rest areas, your desk after work, parked in a safe place in your car, take that nap and notify someone of your location so they can check on you. Take a car service home and come back for your car the next day.

True story: A young lady was out one Saturday night and while driving she dozed for a second. When she realized it, her car was flipping over on the road. It flipped over three times.

Along with the Creator, the seatbelt, and the airbags, she said that she knew to hold the steering wheel tightly because she felt that if she had let it go, she would have been severely if not fatally injured. Rollercoasters have a new place in my heart. That incident could have gone another way completely.

Know your limits, eat well and rest if you know that you are tired. There will be another event on another day. I am grateful to be able to share that story especially with the outcome. The doctors were not sure if her blood count was low, tiredness or exhaustion was the cause. No alcohol or drugs were related.

Hoping that this story will educate and enlighten someone else. Life experiences are to be shared as these lessons can prove life saving for the next person. You can see the picture of the vehicle on the website, SiskIntro.com

There are the occasions when you are led out of situations, relationship, hostile environments, you know, places where you should not be any longer, and you keep returning. You are pulled back in, because of emotional ties, need for security (which it may not be), afraid of what the folks may say, or

Mind Is Too Mental As Teeth Are Too Dental

fear of trying your new direction, your new role, in the next act of your play of life. Whatever your age, recognizing the signs and warnings should be enough to steer you away, and keep you away from what isn't good for you. Pay attention.

There is a season for everything. Not everything is forever. Keep your eyes open for signs that will show you when it's time to end your involvement in certain situations. When you continue to return to the situation, that's called high risk of a bad ending. Stay aware, stay awake and stay in pay attention mode.

Remember, the three strikes you're out scenario, could be you. Adopt the 2 Strike Rule. 1st Strike, you showed me. 2nd Strike, I believe you. That's it!!! Because with the 3rd strike, you're out. Remember? 3 Strikes You Are Out! Don't wait for the 3rd Strike. If you are paying real close attention, you can step out of the situation on the 1st Strike, when there were early signs. No need to wait, when the signs are clear before the 1st Strike.

If it saves your life, or saves you and your family from grief, heartbreak, physical fights, or spiritual fights, step out, as you stepped in, whole, healthy, vibrant, and happy.

If your body, mind, tummy, or financial situation continues to get shaky and unstable, because of the influence of others, those others may not be best for you. Pay close attention to the signs…and follow a direction that shine lights on you.

Be your best you always.

Just Because:

Overeating like hoarding can be dangerous to your health. Just because you think it, you find a way to get it and eat it. Just Because. Not hungry, just ate and because you are thinking about it, you go for it. One of the reasons for this, is high fructose corn syrup which has mercury. It causes a blockage of a chemical called leptin from being released in the body. Leptin tells your brain when you are full. A lack of self-control also exists, because you know that you aren't hungry, that you just ate and still you make every effort to get that something that you are thinking about. This is so you can satisfy your thought of that desired item or items.

These with a host of other factors can cause overeating, obesity and many other health conditions including pre-mature death. So just maybe, creating an eating schedule, choosing foods more wisely and staying hydrated with water, may lead to being healthier by habit. They say do something for thirty days, and it can become a habit. Try something new and see if it's true.

Just Because:

Sometimes people collect without needing. They have a desire to have, just because they think it may be needed at some time. Hoarding can lead to dangerous living conditions, illness, and death by way of accident or disease depending on the condition of the residence. These situations can cause loneliness, sadness, and depression. This condition can also be a sign of something emotional or mental going on. Holding on to family or friends' possessions as a way of feeling close to them, and not giving up on them. Possibly it's a way of not letting go of them.

If they have moved on and we have not, living our life to the fullest has ceased to exist. This can be considered a form of suicide. When one has stopped living completely, due to a loss. Not a good start or finish to a day.

Choices that we make every day can affect our lives and the lives of our loved ones. Take for instance some of the video games. The creators of some of these games have an agenda. Control and money. Mind training, impatience, foreign universal languages, rudeness, and disrespecting others.

Desensitization of murder, killing, anger, death, rape, sacrifice, and racial bias are thoughts and actions being planted into the conscious and subconscious mind of the player.

When playing is not going on, it is being thought of. Like any addiction, these games are not just habitual, they are second to apple pie or burgers and fries for some. Try getting players away from the game without them displaying anger and aggression. It is a hard thing to do. When they are not playing the games and are attempting to engage in real life situations, the mind/mental state is still in the game. Their responses are quick, quick, impatience, rudeness, loudness, and anger.

The amount of money that is spent on some of these games is incredible. Purchasing virtual items just to be competitive in the game. Feeling like if you don't have these items, you are not a part of the "in crowd." It also becomes major peer pressure, which can cause anxiety to develop if someone wants to play, but do not have the gear to fit in. Some people cannot handle these pressures and that's when these ideas then enter and can take control of the persons thinking.

This agent tries to pop in and take control, causing you to try little things to see if they work. Like threatening others in

Mind Is Too Mental As Teeth Are Too Dental

hopes of retaliation. Trying new drinks or drugs because everyone else is doing it. These behaviors have a bad effect on your consciousness. When we know better but do wrong, this can have a negative effect on the mind and body. This is a way of allowing this agent a place to enter and lurk in comfort and it just waits until it finds the proper time to attack.

There are no secrets. When something is done whether it is good or bad and you think that no one knows, well guess what, you know, and it can forever bring you joy, or it can haunt you.

These bad or negative incidents can be true fertilizers for this agent to sprout. They can interfere with your awake hours as well as your sleeping hours. Just think before doing or saying.

Reversal does not happen and forgetting either. Just do not do it! When you decide to do or say something, and your body, your tummy turns and reacts to it, in an uncomfortable way, it just may be telling you that the wrong decision has been made.

Think first. For those of us who know right from wrong, we should do what is right. Ask yourself this question; "How do I want to rest at night, with sleeping pills or a sleeping pillow?"

Mind Is Too Mental As Teeth Are Too Dental

Notes

Mind Is Too Mental As Teeth Are Too Dental

Notes

Mind Is Too Mental As Teeth Are Too Dental

Notes

Mind Is Too Mental As Teeth Are Too Dental

Patience Is Best Used To Understand

Not To Command!

Chapter 5

Everything Happens In Its Time

We are here, on this earth in these bodies for a time. What we choose to do with it, is totally up to us. Well, once we are old enough and or wise enough to make those decisions. Yes, our parents or the adults that we live with, have more control over our lives when we are young, however, to the young people I say; "Change begins in the mind first and planning the best future for yourself, in your mind, can begin the feelings of happiness today."

This is the opposite of telling children to "stop daydreaming." That is what they are supposed to do. Children dream to receive their visions and ideas for their futures. They receive their visions and hopes of what to do next. Adults if lucky are still doing the same thing. The only difference should be that adults daydreaming now, should be accompanied with more knowledge, inspiration, exposure and understanding of what they really want. This is because of their experiences in life. A true fantasy world awaits us all, and it begins in the mind.

Beginning in the mind, how does that help? It's like when you are going on a fun trip or attending a special event on Friday, and it is only Monday. You are so excited that you cannot wait until Friday comes. The anticipation and excitement of what your mind believes will happen on Friday, brings you joy happiness and excitement all week.

People are wondering, why you are smiling so much. Teachers are wondering, why you are behaving so well, and all your assignments are turned in. Parents don't understand why your room is clean and all your chores are done. This is all because of your excitement of what's to come. You do not want anything to interfere with Friday. The same excitement can come with planning your future. Think about it. Pay attention to this type of thinking moving forward.

Today may seem all gloom and doom and other people's lives may appear more exciting. All is good with them. They are happy. Tell yourself this "As soon as I am able, I will do this, and I will do that. My life will take a different turn and I will be, look, and feel happy always." Then get to doing those things which will bring you happiness, and joy today. Step by step.

Everything happens in its' time. Do you agree that what we experience in our lives is about learning and lessons? Not always are the lessons ours. However, we can still learn a little something from them. You can call it sideways learning, or the power of hindsight. Looking back and seeing what has come out of, and how it can help you or someone else. What could have been done differently? How a different choice could have created a different result.

That's what living is all about. We gather our golden nuggets along the way, to create the whole project. Not chicken nuggets, but "gems" of thoughts and experiences leading to our greatness.

Now what would make those experiences better, is if you would share the lessons with others. Those lessons quite possibly could help the next person, should in case they are ever faced with the same, or a similar life issue. They would have your story, your experiences, your lessons to rely upon for guidance. There are no guarantees that all things will go perfectly as planned, but with perfect comes what? Perfect weather. Well go out and play. Perfect song. Well dance until you are tired. Perfect mate. Enjoy every day of it. Perfect job. Hooray that is something to celebrate. Find the perfect for you and your life, which will make you a happier person. Perfect or not, life, with all that comes with it, is worthy of the journey.

 Perfect needs action to make it perfectly what you want and need it to be. Remember, it is your life to make your way. Everything happens in its time, just wait and be here. The time will come that you will see why all things have happened the way they have.

Listen to "Conversations with God" online. It is a bit revealing and relieving. It is "food for thought". It may have some of the answers that you are seeking, in a most inspiring way. Listen to it with friends, and then have group discussions about it.

Do the same with this book, read it and discuss it with family, children, and friends. Create exercises to help work things out. Not everything that we do will give us the results we are hoping for immediately. With the right plan in mind and preparation, you may begin to live a more defined, rewarding and fulfilled life.

Again, this comes with lessons that you will reflect on and share. Keep steadfast in your thinking about what is best for you. Picture yourself there, enjoying the scenes that you set for your life.

Remember, it all begins in the mind first. That is why, it is so important, to feed your mind wisely, with your plans for a long happy and fulfilled life. So Go For It!

Mind Is Too Mental As Teeth Are Too Dental

Time does not really exist in the sense of minute by minute with limits.

It exists based on when it started.

However, it never really ends.

It is on and on and on and on....

So

Be In It

Stay In It

Learn From It

Enjoy It!

Mind Is Too Mental As Teeth Are Too Dental

Notes

Mind Is Too Mental As Teeth Are Too Dental

Notes

Notes

Mind Is Too Mental As Teeth Are Too Dental

Notes

When the only vehicle you have, is a "leap of faith",

Get in and take the ride!

Go For It, Faith works!

Chapter 6

Transformation... The Change

Who? What? Where? When? Why? How? and Are You Sure?

Questions always lead to answers, and yes, you can question and answer yourself. It is okay, despite what they tell us. Feed yourself with thoughts of pleasure. With ideas of greatness. Read "right", listen "right", communicate "right", and talk "right." Keeping yourself in the company of goodness, or no company at all. Self-time is a good time, for reflection time, and the right time, is your time and now.

When we are ready to make changes in our lives not everyone will agree with the change because they are not as ready for the change as you are. You had the time to plan this change. So be kind and patient while sharing your plans with others. This time is not about hurting anyone, causing pain, or placing blame. It's about changing your life for the better.

Keep in mind that even if you are a twin, "you" were born either first or second and given your gifts, strengths, and wisdom, during your arrival, that is specifically for you. As your gifts develop you will be able to share them and yourself with others.

This is self-evaluation time. Who are you? Who have you become? Who did you think you were going to be? How and what do you feel has contributed to you, being the way, you are today? Seeing life, the way you do, why is it so? Did the music of your childhood affect who you are and how you think?

The shows and movies you watched, how have they affected who you are today? What about the books that you have read, did they affect your thinking? Did you observe anyone else's lesson, and learn from that lesson? The people who taught you, like your parents, teachers, and relatives, were they influential to who you are today? Do you remember the adults from your past? Were they kind and patient, or angry and mean? Do you feel that any of these answers, may have affected your life, and the way it is today?

How do you see yourself as you self-evaluate? Are you wise? Are you a patient person? Are you inquisitive? Are you a neat and organized person? Are you a funny person? Are you stubborn? Are you trustworthy? Are you a jealous person? Competitive? Argumentative? Quiet? Humble? Creative? Question who you are to you. Then see how these answers may have impacted your life decisions.

Now use others and ask them some of those same questions about you. Ask them more questions. See who really knows you, the way that you know you. Find out how they see you, during this process. This will also allow you to see who may or may not necessarily be with you in your new life. People that we have known for a long time, do not always know us best. They know us how they see us, based on how they view life. All things may appear good but are not. They may appear bad but are not. What determines this, is the vision of that person's mind, and how their thinking process works.

Well, this can work the same with all people, including professionals who may be evaluating or treating you. How they view life, is how they will see others in their present situations. Their view is not always correct; however, you may get valuable information from their conversation, to help put more of your life's puzzle pieces together.

Here is an example of how different views can work. Four people witnessing an accident. Each one is standing on, one corner of a four-corner intersection. They each have a different version of the how the accident happened. Why? This is because they each see the accident from a different angle.

Their version of the accident is based on how they view things, what their experiences have taught them, and this includes how they process information. Try an exercise with friends, who all see or hear the same thing. Then ask them to explain it in their own words. Don't laugh and don't be surprised. Expect their versions to be a bit different. This should be a fun exercise.

Mind Is Too Mental As Teeth Are Too Dental

You can be living your life with this sneaky sneak, the mind/mental health conditions, imbedded in you. Some of the actions you are taking may be questionable toward your success and happiness being fulfilled. You may not see it, because it may appear normal to you. You may not have a clear view of what is really going on in your daily life. Less clarity about the people that are involved in it.

At the same time, you may be on track with your original plans for your future, but some daily activities may need to be adjusted, for better direction and success. Your daily actions and the actions of those who you are involved with, may be counterproductive to your success. Like, they are in the neutral category. Not for you. Not against you. Just not moving with you toward a success filled, happy life.

While asking yourself some of these questions, and self-evaluating can help to clear your view, this process can provide guidance on how to put your life on track the way you want it to be.

Remember, this is and always will be "Your Time"! This is your time for change. Will others be affected?

Absolutely. Will they live through it? Absolutely. In time, with talk and patience. For you to live the life that you are headed to, you must realize that it is "your time" to shine. Your love for you out powers and out-weighs the love you have for anyone else, while you put this new act in place. This is not selfish by the way; it is self-preserving. There is a difference.

If you are feeling unfulfilled, sad, and or are considering becoming a victim of this agent and letting it win, THEN, RIGHT NOW, RIGHT THIS MINUTE, YOUR FEELINGS AND YOUR HAPPINESS IS WHAT YOU MUST FIND! YOU ARE #1, NO. 1, NUMBER 1, NÚMERO UNO! GOT IT?

You Are The Priority today and always. Keep in mind that if you are not 100% you cannot give 100%. So be all that you can be. Do what you can, to get there and stay there. Keep in mind, that this time, is for you. Be your best at whatever you are doing, and look to you, to keep on doing. It takes work to be all that you want to be.

That's life! So Go Work it!

You do not need anyone else to approve your decision.

Mind Is Too Mental As Teeth Are Too Dental

You need preparation with a plan. You need to focus on what is next. Ask and proceed with these questions and your answers:

What are your options? Who do you want to be? Where do you want to live? What climate is best for you? Do you need a passport, or a full tank of gas? Do you need to learn a new language, or pretend you cannot speak at all? Quiet time is sometimes a blessing.

Set up, in your mind, your new life. All the things that you want to see, hear, feel, eat, and touch, moving forward. That is what you want to be thinking about. What do you want to see each day when you awaken? When and how, do you want to wake up, to start your day? Is it when the clock sounds? Is it when your internal clock says, "okay now... stretch and arise?"

What sounds do you want to awaken to? Will it be the sounds of birds chirping or sounds of ocean waves? Sounds of the leaves, because of the swift breeze, cool air, and the sharp winds. How about awakening to your favorite music? You have choices when you are in charge, of your life. At the end of your day, before you close your eyes to sleep, how should it sound? What do you want to hear?

Get a sound machine or an app that will give you those sounds. It is all within our reach, what we need to improve life. Not just for us but for others as well.

Secret...ssshhhhh...when you awaken...lay for 10-20 minutes reviewing your visits, your dream, or dreams. See where they are leading you for the day. Think about the meanings or messages in your dreams. Are they giving you more direction for your future? Just lay still and relax.

The same again at the end of your day, when you lay in bed to sleep, let it be in quiet, so that more melatonin can be released. Let your brain process your day, and your body replenish itself. Review your day, your journey. Let it pass as rest and sleep arrives.

Or listen to 432 mhz, a relaxation frequency, on a device while you are lying and relaxing. Positive vibrations will come your way. It's a nice feeling... Relax and good night...Now what's next? Where do you go from here? How will you get there?

There is more than one way to end life as we know it. Just

stay here and embrace the better, more exciting, and adventurous options before you.

Now this decision may require you to live in a different part of the world, or just in a different neighborhood. You may need to associate with different people, or no one at all. You know, to do your own thinking. Go back to the old fashioned who, what, where, when, why, and how routine. The answers to those questions may help put you on track.

Here are a few questions to begin with. Make some of your own. Example questions:

Who…is the most important person in my life? You!

What…can I do daily to make myself happy?

Where…is the best place, I have visited, lived, or would like to?

When…was the last time, I considered MY desires?

Why…has it taken me so long to assess my friendships?

How…could I make my life better now, and in my future?

Look at your resources. What resources you ask? Well, if you are the owner of whole life insurance policies on you or someone else, and they have cash or loan value, then who better to use some of that money than the one who has paid into it for years?

If you have a pension plan or other types of investments, you should have access to the funds, either by cashing out or taking a loan against it. This may also be the answer if you are facing financial difficulties. Look at your resources and bail yourself out, with your own money. Step by step. For a better life.

Note: If you are divorced but still want the beneficiary to be your divorced spouse, you must re-assign that person to your policy as beneficiary, after the date of your divorce.

This is especially important if the owner of the policy is the spouse, who may have been paying the premiums on the policy, and if there are other children from other relationships involved.

Protect all your loved ones equally. Divorce isn't defined by hate. Watch my video on how to have a happy divorce, and having the same ingredients, as having a happy relationship._ YouTube.com@evadynesmith3986_Now there may be other options. If you own a home, consider getting an equity loan, refinancing it or if you qualify for a reverse mortgage, that is an option as well. Reverse mortgage allows you to withdraw some of your equity without having to pay it back (unless you want to).

Once your mortgage is paid off, you must pay your real estate taxes on your own. Which is very important to know. Tax liens are a major problem that most Senior Citizens face.

They don't realize that they are responsible to pay the taxes themselves once the mortgage is satisfied with the bank. That is how tax liens and other utility liens build up. Reverse mortgage and whole life insurance, cash value, can help with these bills.

Again, if you choose to get a reverse mortgage, I recommend that you get a term life insurance policy to cover the equity and interest on the equity that you withdrew. This will assure that your home remains with your family, your heirs, when you are naturally no longer here. If it is important to you, to have family retain the home. Let your money work for you!

Check if a Transfer Of Deed (T.O.D) or a Trust is available where you live, along with the reverse mortgage, and for estate planning. These items will help.

If you are going to relocate, consider renting your house or selling it, if you do not plan to return to it, and provided there are no children in the home who will become displaced. Look at the ideal place that you want to live or spend an extended vacation, and check the purchasing, renting, sharing or exchange programs that best suits you.

It's your time. Review your resources and see how far they will get you. Not just away from your current world that you no longer want to live in, but in the long run.

Will your resources hold you for six months to one year financially? Should you seek a new job before you go? Register with temporary employment agencies, or let your union know that you are relocating, to see if they can place you in a position. Consider finding stand-up comedy and open mic venues in the area that you live in now, and in the area that you want to live, because guess what, you may need to laugh, cry, and or tell your own story, which may be a gift to someone else.

Mind Is Too Mental As Teeth Are Too Dental

Use the internet today to watch, listen or see anything that you use, to like, or that you like now. This can happen at any time, any place, and anywhere, that you are located. The internet is a long and winding road that offers global reach without a passport.

Did you know that it could be so easy to get a good laugh, or see a favorite tv program from your past, that you really enjoyed? Did you know that you could take classes, learn languages, connect with old friends and acquaintances, right from where you are sitting today?

Do you like cruising? Apply to work with the cruise lines. Like flying and being up in the air? Consider becoming a flight attendant or register for pilot school. It is never too late to start over, or to start a new career or hobby. Find your passion and try to find a job in your passion area.

There is nothing more rewarding, and there is nothing you cannot get paid to do. Want to travel at discount prices?

Check out the travel link in the appreciation gift. Fam trips are a perfect way to travel for less. Soul search, deep inside for your passion. That something that you love doing every day. Look at what your professional life has been and see if you can make it a business. Market your services to the non-profit community, to help others with your skills. You can find funding for your services, and offer a whole package to organizations or corporations, that you will be paid to provide. How fun would that be?

Get help from people that you know to establish your new career. There is so much power in people if we just open up to share and receive. The energy is there. Just ask, and people who are willing, will share with you. This energy can take your plan to the next level. Be willing to share information, whether you are asked or not. That is the individual power in every one of us.

Networking For Success is our earthly responsibility.

Are you a professional and the pressures of your work life got you down? Find work in a different field, one that you may be over-qualified for, but satisfies your needs financially. If you need to move around and you like people, apply to work at a supermarket or in the retail industry doing something different like managing, stock clerk or cashiering. Clock in, work, clock out, no pressure. Or become a restaurant host or server. Clock in, work, clock out, no pressure.

Well, both examples are physically challenging, because you are on your feet a lot, but hey you may need that too. Get paid to exercise. Why not? Lol

Have you been unemployed for a while and it's hard to find a job or get hired? Apply for a government program and enroll in their work or training program. Then, when you start looking for work again, with more skills, and you have a government program, you may get hired quicker because the company will receive tax credits for hiring people who receive assistance, including unemployment.

Are you sick and tired of an illness that have you feeling down and out? Maybe a little hopeless? You may want to consider finding another source of treatment with less pharmacy medications. It just may be the medications causing you to feel that way. Those feelings are usually listed as side effects of certain medications. Those feelings could also be caused by the combination of medications interacting with each other. Which is another issue because it creates other issues.

Speak to your Doctors and Pharmacists about the interactions of your medications. They should all give you, tell you, explain to you, the same information. Then, you should research it yourself and compare the information that you have received. Be aware of what you are taking and how you are expected to feel, short and long term.

Remember to ask, "how will this medication work in my body and how effective has it been for others. What are the side effects?"

Again, keep in mind that if you are having these feelings, this could mean that the sneaky sneak is lurking around your life. This doesn't mean that you invited it. It's not necessarily your fault. It could be caused by one of the accessories. Outside influences can have an impact on your thinking. Your food and nutritional intake or chemical imbalances may be causing protein deficiencies, thereby causing your neurotransmitters in the body to miscommunicate needed information to keep you in a happy functional place.

Try Chinese Herbal Doctors, acupuncture, Naturopathic Doctors, plant and food-based vitamins and nutritional products. You can find some of the best information and product choices on this website, under "Nutrition and Wellness", www.networkingforsuccess.info .

Here are some examples; Invite Health, Dr. Raymond Omid, Remedies Herb Shop, QueenAfua.com or YahkiAwakened.com You have the time so use it.

Cleansing the body helps to provide clarity of thought, and your decisions will become more focused. Include the teas for parasite detoxification. As we eat, drink, and breathe daily, we take in little molecular items that are airborne and can destroy our systems without our permission. A good detox can help rid the body of those unknown visitors.

Even when you are sick with a cold or flu, when you are taking over the counters or prescriptions, it is good to take a mild laxative to help rid out what is being killed. This helps to get waste out of your body. Changing linen and spraying daily can help you feel better, through your healing process as well.

When you get to the part of cleaning out your whole body, go deep. Just like you do, when you are washing your hair, or preparing to wash the laundry. You gather all the products needed to completely get the job done. This is so that everything is cleansed the way you want it to be. Did you know that your brain cleanses itself when you are asleep? Did you know that your body repairs itself while you are asleep? Look it up.

That leads me to wonder why when hospitalized, you are awakened so often for this or that. During this sleep time, your body is doing its thing of regenerating new cells and going through its own process for healing. This may also explain why, while in a coma, sometimes the body has a chance to relax and heal itself. It is in a deep sleep which allows for natural healing to happen when possible.

Once you begin making changes, you may like the path that your life is taking. You may have needed some life cleansing, to get you back to or introduced you to, where you are going to be your happiest. That includes the mind body and spirit. The whole body. The holistic approach. Internal and external, inside, and outside.

Everything that we do, should be done with thought. The question is, "what are we thinking with?" Is it bad energy, or good energy? Good vibes or bad vibes? Bad company good company or no company at all? Find your good space to think about what your next steps should be.

Are you thinking that this life is not for you? Well, you may be right. If so, go find it. Find the life that you know should be yours. The one that you should be living. The life that you want to be living, right here on Earth. This is the life that you want to live, love and be happy with. That is the key.

Now, that is change in a way that you can live through and absolutely love yourself afterwards. It takes strength to make changes that you can walk ahead with. It is not always easy, it is not always hard, but when you reach your desired results, it is so worth it. So, start here and You will see.... The journey is yours...Transform and Change...

I humbly ask our Creator to please protect our minds, bodies, hearts, souls, and spirits to be able to sustain good health and wellness.

To please give us the strength and the ability to reach out and talk to someone about our feelings, when not feeling good.

I ask that we not be afraid to share life's lessons, good and not so good, so that our experiences can be a benefit to others.

I ask that we take the time to record or write down our feelings, as a way of clearing our minds and our souls, so that our bodies can remain whole.

I ask this for all humans and humankind alike.

Thank You

Evadynè

Mind Is Too Mental As Teeth Are Too Dental

Notes

Notes

Mind Is Too Mental As Teeth Are Too Dental

Notes

Mind Is Too Mental As Teeth Are Too Dental

Notes

Chapter 7

Being Happy

Listen to the lyrics of the song Happy by Pharrell Williams. Do you feel that way? Can you feel that way? Like you are in a room without a roof? Knowing that the sky is not the limit? Can bad news come along, talking this and that, and you let it slide off your body like wet warm spaghetti? Can you see the Sun through the Clouds? The rain as a beautiful cleansing shower...to get started again, with all the past washed away?

Because life happens in ways that we do not always understand, we must stay prepared for it and all its possibilities. Let it be and, make the best out of it. What may be bad, let it be gone and, the good hang around. In all, remember, there are lessons for someone to learn from and not necessarily you.

So, how are you expected to be happy with all that is going on with you, and with this world? How, is the question. The answer is "happiness comes from within". It is about your life. The people you choose to like. The things you like to do. To eat. The way you like to have fun. Your music choices. Your favorite dances. The arts. Watching or playing your favorite sports. Those are your "how" choices! Just think about it.

Happy Thoughts. Think of the best place you have visited on vacation or would like to visit. Who are some of your favorite people, at any age that you can remember? Think about the fact that you can still remember. That is something to be happy about. Use your device to virtually visit anywhere in the world. You can do this today. Right Now. Even without car fare.

There are reasons to be happy, because happy is within first. No one can take that away. It is valuable, and a wealth that cannot be spent. You can however borrow some happy from others, while still leaving the root of happiness for the owner. Like Braco the Croatian Gazer, a

144

human tornado, lifts gifts from people, to share with others. He drops the gifts on those who need it, and the effect is there.

The lessons…remember? If you know someone who always seems happy, genuinely happy, naturally happy, talk to them, and ask them the, who, what, where, when, how, and why questions about themselves and their forever happy outlook on life. Once you have this formula for happiness, inner joy and peace, you can never go broke. Your happiness will be abundantly clear. You can always reach in and grab a bunch of happy thoughts and overshadow what may be coming to cloud your joy.

Find your happiness today and hold on to it tightly. Do not let it go. Be selfish and stingy now. Don't let anyone take away your dreams and happiness. Dream stealers could be the closest people to you. Evaluate the people in your life honestly. Not, who you want them to be, but for who they really are.

Can you relate to the lyrics of Just Fine by Mary J. Blige? "Just Fine?" Feeling just fine, liking what you see, when you're walking past the mirror. Remember when that was you? Or is this you now? No matter how long ago it may have been, just try to remember that time when you had happy feelings.

Keep that picture in your mind. Get back to it or add to it. To living in a happy space mentally, and then physically, will follow. No choice.

Your mind is genuinely great, powerful, and full of energy. Use it to keep your happy in a reachable place. Which means keeping it clear of unhappiness.

Until you find that happy place physically, which may take time, keep your space, your mind, on your happy thoughts. From waking up, throughout your day, and into your night. Keep your "happy in mind." Keeping up the inside first and outside will follow.

Does that mean everything is perfect...NOPE.... just perfectly on its way to where, you are "happy" all the time and your everything is "just fine."

Food For Thought: Keep in mind that what you take in, is possibly, what you will be made of. If you watch

Mind Is Too Mental As Teeth Are Too Dental

negativity listen to negativity, read negativity, then your life may mimic that type of energy. When you must walk that long block, to the store, ss it a long block, or the store at the end of the block? How will you focus on the journey? Like the glass being half full or half empty? How do you look at things?

This type of thinking will determine how happy you see yourself being, and what it will take to get you there. The power of thought. The law of attraction.

If you understand this and if you want to test it, start listening to, reading, and watching more uplifting media content, clean comedy, easy on the mind music, musicals, and love stories. Identify someone that you enjoy hearing speak, based on the sound of their voice, or the "movement of their voice", and listen to them on a device. Just try these ideas.

Examples: I enjoy listening to, Dr. Michael B. Beckwith, he has a voice that I find very nice and easy to listen to and his messages are very uplifting and inspiring. You may know him from The Secret, The Agape International Spiritual Center and Rythmia.com. The power is within us all. Once released, it will have us living, truly living, in a more special place, here on Earth. Who, I ask, does not want that type of living today and every day? Peace, joy, and happiness. Look him up and enjoy.

Also, Pastor Joel Osteen speaks very nice. His voice sounds like he is reciting poetry. He too, has very uplifting messages. The flow and tone of his voice makes him very easy to listen to. He tells stories that are relatable to real life, based on biblical scriptures. These stories may be good for someone listening at the time, and a light of hope may shine on them, for them or someone they know.

You don't have to be religious to receive good messages.

Look at this example of powerful silence. Braco is a Croatian Gazer. He does not speak in the work that he does, but his energy speaks volumes. He gazes; stares left, right, and center, at the audience, and awesome things happen for the people who are in his presence. In silence, no speaking verbally, at all, he gazes.

I see him as a human tornado. I believe that his energy lifts the gifts of others and shares them with those who need it. Not taking it away from the owner, but through spirit and energy he lifts the value of a persons' gift, and places it where it is needed. The life changing testimonies and stories from those who have experienced him, are so inspiring. Look him up and experience him for yourself.

Again, not everything is for everyone. From a different perspective, he can help bring messages clearer, in the minds of those listening or being in his presence. In the case of Braco, you are being present in the right place, at the right time, with the right energy to connect, with your goals and dreams. Who could ask for anything more?

It is like getting advice of two hundred words from one person, and it being more valuable than twenty thousand words from another. This is because, where the receiver is, in their mind space, at the time of receiving the 200 words of advice. The space that was available for those pieces of the puzzle to fit. All that we need to know, is that true happiness is found within oneself. Putting the puzzle pieces in place can make it all complete.

In the case of personal relationships, it is not good to look for someone to make you happy. If you are not happy within yourself, you are not coming to the table with your half in place. If you look for others to bring you happiness, what will happen when they are no longer there? Well, away will go your happiness and your joy. That is not the result you were planning for, nor expecting, for a happy life.

Be as happy as you can be, all the time. Make your happy with your ingredients and then you can invite guests. Having someone add to your happiness and your joy is wonderful. It is a compliment. The other person should be bringing their joy and happiness as well. If someone tells you, "I need you to make me happy". RUN!

Everyone should bring their happy to the table, when they are coming to start a relationship. Getting started on the right foot. Equal additions. Teamwork.

There are a few people that we should want to make happy. Who should we want to make happy? We want to make children happy by exposing them to the wonderful things that life has to offer them. Loving them. Sharing learning activities and fun things, that brings them joy and lots of laughter. They need vacations and adventures to be shown to them, because all experiences will become

Mind Is Too Mental As Teeth Are Too Dental

important when it is time for them to make their own choices in life.

Keep in mind, that what you say to children can stick with them forever. As we talk about happiness and being happy, please do not tell children to "stop daydreaming." They have no bills. No responsibility of taking care of others. No job to worry about. So why not dream. As they are daydreaming and receiving their blessings for their todays and their tomorrows.... LET THEM DREAM ON...

Making happy also, should be our Parents, Senior Citizens, and all Caregivers, because they deserve to see goodness in those whom they have invested their lives and their time. Their time and effort was to prepare the young ones for their own future success. To know and see the results of their lessons, will show them that the lessons they have taught have been received well.

Some have made sacrifices on behalf of their children because it was their choice to become Parents, which made the welfare and happiness of that child, their responsibility. A selfless pleasure it must have been to share life and vacations, music and literature, museum visits and family gatherings with the children in their lives. This should have made everyone happy.

Last to mention, but first and best of course, would be You.

You want to be happy in all that You do, which in turn will shine on others. And about daydreaming...We may want to try to remember some "daydreams" from our past, present and leading into the future,,,,

Dream On.........

Just saying...

Mind Is Too Mental As Teeth Are Too Dental

Make a list of happy times, thoughts, and ideas from your
Past and Present that can lead into your Future, and keep
them handy…

Mind Is Too Mental As Teeth Are Too Dental

Notes

Mind Is Too Mental As Teeth Are Too Dental

Notes

Notes

Mind Is Too Mental As Teeth Are Too Dental

Notes

HAPPY is yours to have and to hold,

From this day forward....

Happy Starts With You!

Chapter 8

Family and Friends Having Their Say

Sometimes they know us and sometimes they just do not. Just because they were raised with you or grew up with you, it does not always mean that they really know or care about you. They don't necessarily know how you are feeling, and what you are going through. We keep a lot to ourselves. Some of which, we should be speaking to others about. Journalizing the things that are happening in our lives is good, because it helps us to get a lot of things off our minds, in that certain kind of way.

When speaking about your issues, you can pretend that it is a friend you are speaking about, when explaining the situation to someone. This will be, to get feedback without the person knowing it relates to you. Like when you are having a difficult day with some co-workers who are a bit odd in the way they act, despite their age. Well sharing that information with a friend, may give you an idea of how to handle it without getting yourself all worked up...at work.

We should not assume knowledge and maturity comes with age. Age is automatic. Our experiences, as we are developing into adults and our ability to process and act appropriately on those experiences, is not so automatic. Age and expectations of the aged, can be misleading and disappointing.

Once we realize this, we will not be confused when we encounter adults who act like they don't know any better. We may then hesitate before saying, "You would think they would know better at their age." Age is automatic, experience is not. Now we know better!

When speaking to someone that you know, about your situation, keep that lesson in mind. Reflect on your knowledge of them, and if they are the right person to have this conversation with. You are looking for resolution and clarity, not idle chatter Never expect from someone what they have never showed you they could deliver. If you do, and they don't deliver, you would have let yourself down. They didn't let you down. Even if they agreed to it. They meant well, and may have tried their best, but was unsuccessful. Remember, it was your expectation of them, not what you knew they could succeed at.

Having their say:

When speaking to friends and family about your new plans, some may feel it isn't a good idea. Judgement can happen. Be mindful of the lesson, that common sense isn't that common at all. People will see through their eyes and process based on their understanding of life. That does not make it yours or what is best for you.

When and if, this sneaky sneak stalks you, and brings forth all the things going on in your life, and invites you out of it, tell "it" to take a leap...SAY NO and GO AWAY.

Journalize what you were thinking or doing before this thought creeped in. Begin to journalize your food intake, and your activities. Include your sleep pattern as well. All these things matter when you are monitoring yourself. Understanding how your body reacts under certain conditions will be discovered with these exercises. We are always learning as long as we are living. (t) That is the plan.

Call someone and talk things out. Yes, people can be judgmental at times, of a person's actions and sometimes harshly but just listen, carefully. Save the valuable pieces to add to your puzzle. Leave the rest in reserve because you never know if it will be needed later.

Talk to three or four people throughout the week and hear what they have to say. Place in your basket what is good for you. Same here, with the remarks that you may receive from others. Out of three thousand words, two hundred may be useful. Use them wisely. Keep your reserve just in case. While on your journey, of this changed life, that reserve may come in handy.

Remember, because this is, "save a life, time", there is no room for extra baggage. This is the time that you will get feedback from several people that you know, on how you are feeling. How you are doing. How you are acting.

Mind Is Too Mental As Teeth Are Too Dental

Suggestion, try not to speak to all green people. Find green, yellow, and gold people. Pick different types of people, from those that you work with, play with, travel with, and live with. See how well they understand, see, and know you. You will want to listen to them carefully to pull out the golden nuggets.

When and if you make this decision to change your life, there are some special people that you may want to talk to. Your Parents, whatever their age, may not understand your decision. It is okay. You want to put it together in a way for them to receive it, without criticizing them. You want to bring them to a place of comfort with your decision and why you have made it.

Some adults have not realized yet, that we are all people, no matter the age and relationship. That a fair and even exchange of respect and appreciation is due to all. Some believe they are owed something for birthing and or raising their children. They do deserve something for sure, something like having a happy child and ultimately a happy adult who was once a child.

If no one has ever, let this be your first or hopefully added to the rest, A GREAT BIG THANK YOU. This comes your way for being a parent, auntie, uncle, grandparent, teacher, and anyone who took responsibility for overseeing the growth and development of a child. That is a big job, without real training. Keeping in mind that each child is an individual and no matter how many you have, or how often you are blessed to help nurture, raise, teach, and prepare a child for future life, no two are the same.

Again, without training, it can be a big and beautiful job to undertake. Let's agree that the greatest gift of all, is a happy child or adult after years of guidance and love. A child, young or old who is on track to their success. Not a track of escaping a controlled environment and taking whatever first offer comes along.

Instead, you should want someone who deliberately investigates their options and makes the best decision for themselves. That is why exposure to life's great wonders is especially important for children. It will help when they are in position to make their own decisions. When the parents aren't around. This is long before adulthood. This is school age, on the playground, or anytime thereafter. Right?

Mind Is Too Mental As Teeth Are Too Dental

Your decision to change your life, as a living person, may be hard for everyone. Family and friends to begin with.

But letting any or these agents make you a victim would be even harder. So go ahead and make your decisions. Make your plans. Set them forward and remember, "when you decide and start living in your decision, your life gets better from that point on."

This is even before you tell anyone anything. Before you relocate. Before you even make your first call. In your mind, your new life, your happiness has begun. In your mind, is where all greatness begins. Every day will get better and better. Be here to see it.

Having these communication sessions with your people is also useful, because in all that you discover, you may discover that a simple message, was misunderstood. This could be due to a device completing the spelling of words and the message being sent, and no one questioning it. Just accepting it and acting accordingly. Bad feelings caused by a misunderstanding, can begin. This caused tension or disagreements, and no one clarified the message.

Wow… Double check your messages before sending.

We must start communicating directly again, or for some, start communicating period. Whatever method of communication you use, verbal TTY or ASL, use it to avoid confusion. This of course could mean not texting.

Sorry, I know that is hard to think of for some. Lol. Make sure that you are clear when you speak to someone. Know that your message is understood, as clearly as you wanted it to be.

Please communicate if something bad has happened. Whether or not it is your fault, but somehow you are liable. This may be personally, financially, or maybe professionally. Please have a clear conversation about it with your spouse, friends, and family members. Liquidate your resources to correct the problem if it is financial or promise to correct it soon.

Whatever you do, do not let this create a stressful situation. You could have a stroke, or heart attack, from the pressure. Don't be led to killing your family members, or anyone else, and possibly then yourself. That is not the answer. This is not how life should be. Find a way to correct the issue, even if it means that you must start all over in your career. You will have a jumpstart because you now have more experience to start with. Mistakes happen. Bad decisions happen. Life ending, does not get a chance for reversal.

As a thought, require two signatures for withdrawals from family resources. Gambling problems can cause families to lose their valuable properties, life savings and then life itself by others or can cause life ending thoughts to oneself. Just saying.

The idea of not wanting your family or friends to suffer for something that you are responsible for, shows the amount of love that you have for them. So don't hurt them in any way. Suicide is such a disheartening event. Murder then suicide will affect more lives forever. Loss of life should never be the option when there are ways to correct the problems.

Seek ways to change a situation. This action destroys many lives, young and old, near and far and for a very long time.

Revenge is not the answer. If someone has done something that hurt you badly, stand up and acknowledge the hurt to yourself. Don't try to hide it. Emotions can become uncontrolled human explosions. You can however, control this by communicating how you feel. The stronger you are and the way you will process it, and then rebound will show the real you. The you that you are inside.

Take a deep breath before responding. This will allow an opportunity for you to process the information received and decide if it needs a response. Many times, it does not.

Deep Breath. Deep Breath. Deep Breath.

We are always growing to become. So don't let the actions of others control you. Revenge, anger, and most emotions are processed through the liver. You don't want to make yourself sick, with planning and plotting. Move on with the lessons learned from that experience and become the better You. The bigger You. The healthier You. Inside and out.

Life Experiences:

Some people may have taught You, but that's because You were capable of learning. You. Someone may have helped You promote on the job, but that's because You were

Mind Is Too Mental As Teeth Are Too Dental

qualified. You. Someone may have proposed marriage, You said yes, then they changed their mind. You say thank you for the opportunity to be engaged, and I will move on with the good memories of knowing how it feels to love someone. You.

Someone close to you appeared to be a friend then showed themselves to be disloyal and disrespectful to the friendship. To that You say, glad to have had the lesson. I hope that you stay well. Now that I know your true colors. I will keep you in the box of crayons where you best fit. You.

We cannot make people do or feel anything. We can make sure that we check off, on our list, our points of what true humanism is. Check that our senses and emotions are well intact, as being a good human being. Check that our feelings are correct and in good working condition, to know when we are not being treated fairly. With that knowledge and understanding we move on knowing what is possible from that person. Check Mate!

Communication is the real key...keep it open...keep it working...it works.

Notes

Mind Is Too Mental As Teeth Are Too Dental

Notes

Notes

Mind Is Too Mental As Teeth Are Too Dental

Notes

Notes

Friends tend to know us differently and sometimes better than family, because there is a common relationship with friends.

Friends are chosen.

Family is given.

That's Valuable….

Chapter 9

Don't Forget To Say Goodbye

Stop this agent in its tracks and eliminate the possibility of it being a winner in your life. This chapter offers suggestions on how to say goodbye to the old and unwanted, while moving forward in specific areas of your life, as you build a new one. Do know, that you do have a right to build a new one.

The life that you want to leave behind has been handed to you. From your gender to your eye color, your hair texture, the schools you attended, the city you lived in, and who you are in a relationship with. But guess what, now that you know more about yourself, you are entitled to create the world in which you want to live. This is in no way

176

meant to be a display of disrespect to anyone that you love or who loves you. It is a clearer, and deeper respect for your life. Begin to live it the way you want to live it.

Now, how do you start knowing that saying goodbye to your old life is not going to be easy? You must first make the decision and second create the plan, for the changes that you feel will make you the happiest. Making the decision is 50% of the process. Action is the other 50%.

Remember, mentally in your mind, once you make the decision, you can begin living in it. Rehearsing how you will wake up in the morning and the new things that you will do. The new way you will dress, the new foods you will eat. The new way you will wear your hair. All these rehearsals are the beginning of being in your happier place.

Start your departure plans from your old life today by mentally packing all the positive things that you are taking with you. Do not worry if you do not find much, that could be your reason for this changing life stage. Look at your options. Your age. Your income. Your work experience and your financial assets. If you choose to move, where will you live? Do you know someone who will accept you into their home? Do you have the resources to rent another place? Are you going to travel to another town, state, or country?

Remember, in your beginning days you did not have all that you have now. All that you have accomplished since birth. You did not know then, all that you know now. But now, with all that you have seen, learned, and enjoyed, including your experiences, education, exposures to all that you have come across, this part in your life's play, this journey you are now on, you are more equipped to succeed.

To complete this plan, it may take some time. Time to save. Time to identify the area that you want to live in. Time to see where you want to work or what business you will start or restart. Time is time, and since you have it, use it, value it and make the best of it.

Do you have to change your name? If so, can you remain on your same job with this name change? In the same school? Can you recreate "you", in a way where you do not have to give up what you love, and would like to bring with you on this journey? Choosing to keep the things that you like or love in your life, while setting aside the things that are not pleasing to you, is a great task to take on. Make it like an exercise; up, down, this or that…keep or pass on to someone else. This can also mean distancing from some family members and some friends. This is a task that will require a little bit of evaluating. Are they for you, against you or neutral?

Now keep in mind neutral can take away from your energy of moving forward, so evaluate cautiously. Whatever it takes, do it deliberately and with purpose, because the other option leaves no choice and change will happen anyway. Only on a more permanent level.

Keep in mind, this plan is to avoid you being taken away from those who you love, and to keep you in a happier space. In this space, you will have a better understanding of those you know, and where they fit in. So go ahead talk to your friends and family. Let them know how you feel about them. Leave no doubt in their minds and give them a chance to speak, leaving no doubt in your mind, about your feelings.

While saying goodbye does not have to be so direct, it will give your friends and family an opportunity to know more about the new you. They will hear the way you see yourself. Also, at this time you will have a way to evaluate your life through their eyes. Hear how they see you. Keeping in mind they may not be correct in all that they see and say, but there are little treasures that we can pick out of these conversations, that may help put our life puzzle together, in the way it will please us.

This process may also give light to why you are feeling the need for change in general. If you are feeling bad or unsure about anything they are saying, ask the deeper questions that you need answers to. This may be hard, however living in confusion and letting it get the best of you is much harder.

To all ages, know that this time will be the past, when tomorrow comes. As each second of time passes, that incident, those words, are now in the past. All things do not require a response. Take Deep Breaths Take Deep Breaths Take Deep Breaths.

People who you know, will know how you may react to certain situations. Just as you know the same about them, and how they would react to certain situations. That's where control comes in. When people know what buttons to push, for the results they want, they may push them. Be mindful and stay in control of you.

Be very deliberate moving forward, in how you react when

you hear or see certain things. Take a moment to assess the actions of the other person and determine if it needs a response. Determine if the response would even matter and is this a time when you should just stay quiet, remain still, and observe. Take deep breaths and observe. These experiences will be just that. Keep in mind that today is what matters. The present, moving into the future. The past is over, and guess what, you are still here.

Stay in it. Stay Planning. Stay making your changes and please keep in mind, that it is within your mind and heart that you will first find and begin the feelings of happiness. For today and all the tomorrows to come.

Goodbye Old Life....Hello New Life...I am still here. I will be here for a very long time.

Say it and mean it! Say it out loud thirteen times, so that your subconscious can get it one time. That is the rule.

So, if you want it to stick, repeat it again and again…

Mind Is Too Mental As Teeth Are Too Dental

Contact the National Suicide and Crisis Lifeline

Text or Dial 988

Veterans and Active Military Preventing Substance Abuse and Suicide: https://www.linesforlife.org/mhl/ or

Text 838255

The deaf and hard of hearing can contact the Lifeline via TTY.

Dial 711

http://www.suicidepreventionlifeline.org/ GetHelp/LifelineChat.aspx

Suicide Prevention Resource Guide

http://www.sprc.org/resources-programs/program-encourageactive-rewarding-lives-pearls

Association of Black Psychologists

http://www.abpsi.org/find-psychologists

Association of Psychiatry

www.Psychiatry.org

Mind Is Too Mental As Teeth Are Too Dental

OR KEEP READING

Mind Is Too Mental As Teeth Are Too Dental

Notes

Mind Is Too Mental As Teeth Are Too Dental

Notes

Mind Is Too Mental As Teeth Are Too Dental

Notes

Mind Is Too Mental As Teeth Are Too Dental

Notes

Chapter 10

Stop What You Are Thinking

Please read this chapter with an open mind and a mind open. A mind that would understand and accept how worthy you are now and forever.

If you are thinking that you must leave this world today, that your life, as you know it, is not worth living and others that know you agree with You, FIRST STOP talking to them NOW! IMMEDIATELY. They are not looking out for YOU. They are not your friends.

Know that YOU are WORTHY to YOU!

If anyone has made you feel less than worthy, know that you are bigger, better and stronger now, than you were five minutes ago. You may feel like leaving this life because you KNOW better about yourself. That's a good start for the changes that you will be making. You know that the world has a lot to offer. You can pick and choose what pleases you, and what you feel may make you happy.

You know that you are worthy and that you have value. This is beyond what others may say about you. Now let us get your life to where you want it to be. Think about all the goodness that is before you. Even if you must travel, it 'is" for you. Quitting life is not going to help anyone or anything. There is so much more that you can do, while you are here.

Now is the time to find your life. Find the life that you want to live. Not the one you want to leave behind. Start living a new one. Make up your mind about what you want and get it started, today. This is the time to "pack your things and move". If not literally, right now, then in your mind, begin the move, the change, for a better life for you.

You made the decision to leave all of this behind you. Great!

BUT YOU MUST REMAIN IN FRONT OF IT, IN ORDER TO LEAVE IT BEHIND. You must be willing to try something so extreme, that others will be surprised. You may be the most surprised with your life changes. Start with the one thing that You can get, all by yourself. That you do not need anyone to help you with. Find that one happy thought, item, place, or song which can make you smile, laugh, sing, dance, or just plain enjoy. That is the seed by which your future life will grow! By Yourself! First and For Now!

IF YOU ARE A CHILD OR TEENAGER:

Please know that these may be times of hormonal changes, and these times are so under-discussed. Not only are you going through changes, but so are the adults in your life, and no one is preparing you or them for these changes. People do not understand them. They do not recognize them. These changes may show differently in each person. Every day and every night, the changes will bring different occurrences for everyone. Sometimes these changes are unrealized even after the fact. Let us talk about these natural changes today!

TO ALL:

Stay with us! This too shall pass. You have been around long enough to have seen things change every day. For better or worse, they change. Just stick in it and you will look back in a year and be able to talk about this time in your life. Find your happy thoughts from anywhere in your life and hold them close. Not as in, I wish I were there again, but as in, I was there, it was good, and it can be good again, even if in a different way. Believe that it will be good again, with some changes of course.

Life is a revolving circle; around and around we go. Set your path for a better tomorrow and start right now. You need to get air? Go outside and take in some deep breaths. Take 2 or 3 and feel the air. Cannot get out now? Well then open the window and let the breeze come in. Even if it's not a perfect weather day, you are here to experience it.

You can go into the bathroom and take a shower or soak, using peppermint or lavender liquid soap, (nice mix too), for a relaxing aromatic experience. Have neither, go into the kitchen put some cinnamon in a pot and let it simmer and fill the air while you relax. It gets better day by day. Just keep in mind, "your" happy. You can make either of these mixtures in a cup or bowl with hot water and sit beside it while you work, read, listen to music, write, or just simply relax.

Listen to Adele's music. Her music is very therapeutic. Every one of her songs delivers a message. Go and set your path for better tomorrow, and start to take your breaks today, to relax, and regroup. Gather your strengths because this takes lots of strength and you have it. That is why this sneaky sneak has never shown its face until now. Your true inner strength is still within you.

There may be things going on in life which have weakened you just a little, but you are stronger now, and you will be able to conquer these challenges. You are now armed with tools to win this fight. These are tools that you have been using throughout your life. You just have not had to use them in a long time, or in this same way. Time to hook on the tool belt and get to work.

Tell this agent, "NOPE NOT ME, I CAN SEE". Show this sneaky agent that it is your time to live your life, in the way you know how to. Today the thoughts and ideas of leaving this life totally is not an option. As these thoughts are leaving your mind, say goodbye to them forever.

The thoughts have been stopped, removed from your mind and body. They are gone and you are still here! Hello world, I am, and I will be here, so get ready!

Today is your day to begin your transformation into your new life here on earth, and nothing or no one will be in your way.

Mind Is Too Mental As Teeth Are Too Dental

You are getting back in the race. On the happy track. On the living track. Moving right along into your new life. The life you choose to live, with all that you now know.

Parents who are reading this, please have conversations with your children no matter their age*. Read this book together or apart and agree to have discussions about it. Write each other letters and give your views on it. Share information with each other about what you need in your lives to be happier. Write about the challenges that you are facing, and work on them together. Young people have the wisdom and knowledge of those who were here before them, even before us. They are meant to shed light on the lives of the adults they are around, because older adults have taught them well, from near and far.

Mind reading is a gift that not everyone understands or has received. Therefore, open communication is so important to getting life right. Sometimes we do not have a second chance, so take this one and do what you must do, for your life, and those around you. Everyone has something to say, so keep an open mind to hear and listen. Please.

Suicide is a serious the one of the most serious agents of all the mind/mental health agents. They can arise and affect family, friends and oneself, for a lifetime. All from life's many issues, and the thoughts of harm can reach anyone. If at the wrong time, anyone can become a victim.

Eliminate all avenues that these agents can travel from. Protect the lives of those you love today. You cannot undo what has been done or said, but what you can do is acknowledge all that you know is possible and address it in the open. No fighting, no arguing, no placing blame. That is why writing down your feelings, or recording them, and listening to them alone or together with those involved, or a neutral party, will allow everyone to know what is going on, and without interruptions.

A LITTLE BIT OF TEARS NOW vs. A LIFETIME OF TEARS

PARENTS PLEASE NOTE: As adults, we are not as in charge of our children's lives as we think. We are however, in charge of their well-being. It is particularly important to know if their beings are well. That takes listening, not just hearing what they have to say. Listening with no judgement. No placing blame and no redirecting of blame.

Remember, we were all young before. Our experiences were different from our Parents, now it's our turn to listen, receive, process, and try to understand what our young people are going through. Letter writing is a great way to open conversations. What may come out in the letters or conversations may be surprisingly shocking. Happy times that you may not have realized they enjoyed so much.

Friendships that have developed over time. Some information may also be hurtful and a bit unbelievable, but please be willing to believe what your child will say. Denial accomplishes continued pain. (t)

This is healing and understanding time. It is time for changing and saving lives. If they need to be out of your home, accept that, because that just may be what they need to be better and happier in their lives. In time their full lives will be revealed. It is better to know that they are safe, and that their beings are well, rather than unhappy and negative feelings are lurking in their souls waiting to take it over at any given moment.

BACK TO STARTING OVER...A NEW LIFE...STILL HERE....

Now this decision may require you to make some serious and extreme changes. You may want to live in a different part of the world or just a different neighborhood. To associate with different people or no people at all. Then you have a chance for think time. Quite possibly everything may find its place. Going back to the basics again, you know the old fashioned who, what, where, when, why, and how routine. This process will help you find the answers and it will give you some directions that you may need to move ahead with.

I will be repeating in this chapter from a previous chapter because it is important, and you may be skipping around...or just in a more positioned place to receive these ideas for yourself or someone else.

Look at your resources. What resources you ask? Well again if you have life insurance which is not term you may have cash value or loan value. Who better to use your money source, than you, who have paid into for years? If you have a pension plan or investments, you may have access to funds either by cashing out or taking a loan. This may also be a way of clearing your debt or a financial crisis, which may be weighing you down and causing bad stressful feelings in your life.

If you own a home, then you may have the option to take an equity loan or get a reverse mortgage. I suggest that if you get a reverse mortgage, you should get a term life policy, check out the Transfer On Death Deed (T.O.D.) in your area, which will allow your heirs to get your house back into your family's ownership completely, once the debt is paid. You can also refinance it, rent it, or sell it, provided there are no children in the home who will be displaced. Look for the ideal place that you want to live and check out the purchasing, renting, sharing or exchange program that best suits you.

It is **CHANGE TIME** and it does not mean quitting life, time.

"Know That..You Are.. An Example To.. Someone Else" (t)

Pool your resources together and see how far they will get you. Not just away from your current world that you no longer want to live in, but in the long run, in your new life. Will you have enough resources to hold you for six months to one year financially? Should you seek a new job before you go? Maybe register with employment agencies. Let your union know that you are relocating and see what help they can offer.

Find the stand-up comedy and open mic venues in the area that you want to live. Because guess what? Your story is one that may be a gift to someone else and you yourself may need a laugh or two. Or you can start your own online venue to share and share alike. Do you like cruising? Apply to work with the cruise lines. Like flying? Become a flight attendant or register for pilot school. It is never too late to start over in a new career or hobby. Find your passion, work in it. Look at what your work life has been and see if you can make it a business.

Market your services and skills to the non-profit community and help others with the skills that you have. Get help from people that you know, to establish your new career. There is so much power in people and what we have to offer each other. Let us begin to use each other, for the benefit of each other.

Are you a professional and the pressures of work got you down? Find less stressful work. Apply to a supermarket. Become a server in a restaurant if you enjoy people. Have you been unemployed for a while and cannot find work anywhere? Apply and receive public assistance or any government program that you qualify for and go through their work or training program for new skills. Once completed, you can start looking for work again and you may have more success.

If a person is receiving government assistance, a company will get tax credits for hiring them. Companies will usually do what will benefit the company first. Therefore, your chances are higher because of the tax credits that the company will receive.

Mind Is Too Mental As Teeth Are Too Dental

Are you sick and tired of the illness that has you feeling down and out and a little hopeless? Well consider finding another source of treatment with less pharmacy medications, which could be causing you to feel sad, hopeless, depressed, and suicidal. Visit: BeatCancer.org for Cancer Support Coaches and nutritional support while you heal and recover.

Again, keep in mind it is not necessarily your fault if you are having these feelings or thoughts of ending your life. Do not blame yourself. Strap on your tool belt and get busy.

Try Chinese Herbal Doctors, acupuncture, or Naturopathic Doctors. Eat healthy nutritionally rich foods. Use food-based natural vitamins and food-based nutritional supplements. You can find helpful information and links on the NFSPCN.com site or on NetworkingForSuccess.info such as, InviteHealth.com, QueenAfua.com, RemediesHerbShop.com, Namaskar.com, YahkiAwakend.com, Dr. Raymond Omid on YouTube, and following BlackMagik363 on YouTube will direct you to a vast amount of knowledge. All offering valuable information and exceptional products, services, and resources.

If you eat meat and dairy, organic eggs are full of vitamins and minerals and the good cholesterol. Remember the egg commercial jingle, "the incredible edible egg"? It used to be the commercial before the statin drugs became popular. Grass fed liver is full of vitamins minerals and nutrients.

AncestralSupplements.com offers products in capsule form, of various organ meats that are full of vitamins and minerals.

Detox your body if you have the time. Cleansing the body helps to provide clarity of thought and your decisions will become more focused. Include a parasite detox, as we are bound to take in something alive out of the air without us knowing it. Get good sleep and let your brain cleanse and your body heal itself. This should and can be done every day. The brain takes on a lot and works very hard. So let it cleanse, starting with a good night's rest. Everything that we do will take thought. A clear head/mind/mental space is a great start. So be mindful of what you take in.

What are you thinking with?" Is it bad or good energy? Good or bad vibes? What type of company do you keep around you? Are they healthy for you? Are you thinking that this life is not for you? Not the life that you thought you would be living. Well, you just may be right. If so, now is the time to start changing it. Find the life that you know you should be living or want to be living. One that will make you happy. Change begins now.

These are changes in a way that you can live through and love yourself afterwards. It takes strength to make changes. Make the change that you can walk ahead with. It is not always easy, it's not always hard, but it is, so worth it. You will see....

Note* Young people have the gift of knowing. They can help with guidance and direction. Let them into the conversations about life's challenges. Help them, while helping yourself, to better understand life, finances, relationships, respect friendship, you know...life. They will help and be prepared for their future lives as well. It's a win, win!!

Have a conversation with the young ones in your life. They are very wise and knowing despite their age.

Ask them about their future goals. When they share that by age this or that, they want to have enough money to take care of this or that, then you should speak to Me about whole life insurance, to assure that they will reach their desired goals.

Yes, they will do their work to accomplish their goals, but how sweet it will be, when you are able to present them with a deposit, or a nice chunk of change, for what they want, as a reward for their hard work. How and Why…Because todays money can make tomorrows dreams come true. Feel free to contact Me for a" wealth building" review.

Mind Is Too Mental As Teeth Are Too Dental

Notes

Mind Is Too Mental As Teeth Are Too Dental

Notes

Mind Is Too Mental As Teeth Are Too Dental

Notes

Mind Is Too Mental As Teeth Are Too Dental

Notes

Mind Is Too Mental As Teeth Are Too Dental

Get ready for the hardest part.

Exploring and understanding the simplest ways to improve life for us all!

Actions speaking louder than words!

Chapter 11

Elimination:

The Art of Communication

The elimination of suicide and understanding mind/mental health conditions, will begin with the power of communication on all levels until they are gone. We take for granted, these occurrences, until there is another reported case close to us. Then we wish we would have done more seen more or listened more.

Well, I hope that you agree, being ready with tools to keep these agents out of the way is most important. Keeping you, your family and friends prepared to see, avoid and to win against their attack is a priority. As often as we hear about various cases of mind/mental health disorders and suicide actions, we will continue to use our knowledge until they are gone. We will keep doing whatever we have to do, to end the stigmas and the reign, that the word and actions of mental health and suicide have on humanity.

How do we communicate let us count the ways…?

Verbal

Speaking out loud, not loudly about what is going on in your life. If you are being abused or if you are having feelings of being overwhelmed, being annoyed, being threatened, being bullied, tell someone, tell everyone that you are not feeling safe and secure in your space. Do not be afraid of sharing your life experiences with others. The more you share the more we all will learn which in turn equals helping one another. If you keep everything to yourself and if you do not share, the attacker may just win.

Not everyone that you speak with will understand what you may be going through because again there are many ideas, perspectives and past experiences that influence how we see things. The way that our brain processes information is based on those elements. You may be teaching someone something new about you, and as you speak to them about your issue, you may be the one surprised. This reaction can have a positive effect on the situation that you are facing, because the surprise can stimulate more questions from those involved. There begins a conversation.

You do not have to be facing something negative to have these conversations. You could be sharing a happy occasion, a new recipe or dish you may have eaten. A new idea that you came up with or simply happy to be in the day that you are in. Saying good morning, good evening or have a wonderful day to the next person that you see, can make a big difference to all involved.

If someone has come to you with an issue and it is heavy on your shoulders, or your heart, share it with someone. You do not have to mention the name of the person. If it is life threatening, then maybe an authority should get the report. We are all here for the greater good of the next person.

There is an art to listening; it is not just I am here so I cannot help but hear you. It is more like; I hear you and you have my attention, and I am also listening to you. Listening requires attention; it requires you to be in the thought of the speaker. This is listening with intent and giving an attempt to fully understand what they are saying and are not saying.

People at times are so involved with themselves that they only see and hear their points of view. Once they are telling the story, someone else listening can help it become clearer, not only to the listener but also the speaker. Effectively communicating opens up doors.

Hopefully the listener will have an opportunity to ask a question or two. Those questions will expand the story and may help the speaker to realize a solution to the situation, or at least get closer to a better outcome.

It's the art of verbal communication and being in the moment of that conversation, that helps to make it effective. When everyone is engaged in the story and interacting with the information being shared, it becomes more relevant.

Funny how the conversation can start out about one thing and go on and on and lead to so many other topics. Just having the time to engage makes all the difference in the world and to someone's world.

Mind Is Too Mental As Teeth Are Too Dental

Notes

The Arts "Music: Drawing: Poetry: Singing: and Dancing"

Being artistically creative is a most wonderful gift of expression. It is an opportunity to bring out the inner you in a project. The feelings, the visions, the freedoms, the sight beyond seeing, the joys, the pains, the melodies, and the fame. Along with the pleasures that you feel when you see in others, the same expressions on their faces, the movements of their bodies, the tears in their eyes; the roar from their applause and their exhaustion; all the same feelings and expressions that you experienced when creating it. All of this is priceless.

There is joy in using the art disciplines to create from within you. Keep in mind that even if you are not an accomplished artist, you can still do what each discipline requires you to do. You can write your feelings with words that rhyme, or just write and write to pass the time. You can paint or draw from the inside out, with what you feel and see, then watch the colors scream and shout, while your design shows your beauty.

*You could sing so off key that if you wanted, a studio could clean it up for marketing purposes. We have seen that done; but the singing itself is exhilarating. It is freedom of your expression. If you move a little, the feet, the arms, the head, and shoulders, you may have a little something going on there. This all can be done even if you cannot stand, because I have seen some mean chair dancing. This is good for young and old. Just go ahead and find your bold. Everyone can join in. It then becomes a win... win... win.

These expressive art techniques are all possible with no competition, no criticism, and no judgment. You and only you, must approve. Each one of these experiences can truly improve your life. Movements of your body, which is directed by your mind, and guided by the higher power are extraordinary.

Dancing, the watching of it and the doing of it, is powerful. As with dance performances, you can get the story without hearing the words. You can feel the passion and the emotions without hearing the music or knowing who did it or why.

Dancing is all around, no form or fashion and sometimes no music. You are in it one way or another. Watch the movements of people walking on the streets. You can see their movements as they dodge the cracks on the pavement, the people who are passing them, and the traffic as they cross over to the other side. Just watching the movements of their bodies, their heads going back and forth, their eyes keeping a careful watch on what's going on around them. These movements tell a whole lot about how the person is feeling, what they may be thinking and how attentive they are to what they are doing.

How we feel about life, is so important to our everyday living, and to what our futures can hold. The ability to communicate through the arts, is a tool that should be encouraged and continued through all aspects of life, and this includes the school systems. So much can be learned through acting, creative writing, and dance therapy. What are we missing today, without teaching this? Imagine how history and math lessons can be taught and remembered with rhythm attached to it.

Buy an art set or two. Include crayons, pencils, sketch pads, canvas boards, paint, and brushes. Now just get busy. You, your children, your parents. Anyone and everyone can do this expressive exercise. See what comes out of it. A masterpiece? A one-of-a-kind? A couple of limited editions.

Hmm, a limited edition, that's what we all are, you know, limited editions and we each are "one of a kind". Hmm We are Art Treasures.

Mind Is Too Mental As Teeth Are Too Dental

*Note: If you know someone who has a speech impediment due to a stroke or any other condition, try to get them sing what they want to say. Singing comes from a different side of the brain. Practice!

Mind is too mental, as teeth are too dental. It is the state of mind, the condition, the happy and healthy, or not so happy and healthy, that determines the mental state.

Once we learn the different ways to identify the creative parts of our thinking, we will better understand, what some conditions are all about. Hearing voices, write down what they are saying. You could be receiving design messages, or movie ideas. It could be self-therapy, like thinking out loud.

Be creative in your thinking. Explore the artistic side of your brain and exercise it. That singing when you can't talk after an illness, is because one side of your brain is literal, and the other side is creative. Learn more about this and be your best. Share with others, to help them be their best.

Thank you!

Mind Is Too Mental As Teeth Are Too Dental

Notes

Mind Is Too Mental As Teeth Are Too Dental

Notes

Silence

Icebreakers are always a good idea, and this can be done anytime and with anyone. Family friends at work or in school. Without announcing what you are doing, just initiate and move forward. There are some people who just don't know where to get started…but once they do…watch out.

When people are too quiet it can be alarming, especially if they are withdrawn and quiet. Not just I do not want to talk right now, but more like I never want to talk. I never or hardly ever want to interact with the group. I shun away from engagements with people. I always sit by myself at lunch time and close my room or office door.

What they may be saying is, "I really need someone to talk to, because just maybe, too many time-outs as a child, may have led to me to feeling comfortable in this lone space. I want to change, but I don't know where to begin." Or "I am an only, youngest, or oldest child, with many years in between, so most or all my life has been about me doing me. I never had to focus on or consider anyone else because it was just me. I know what I am doing here at work, or in school, or in this relationship, because I have been doing it for so long this way."

Mind Is Too Mental As Teeth Are Too Dental

This type of aloneness may not be the healthiest way of life for a fulfilled life. Especially if the person is part of a team or in a relationship or a parent. Their good qualities can outshine the hidden secret of loneliness. But the loneliness can cause negative outcomes that can affect the person and so many others.

If you see that type of behavior, it may be cause for alarm. Whether this is a child or an adult the behavior should be watched carefully. If they don't have a condition where these symptoms would be expected, then this behavior may need some addressing. Even with a diagnosed condition, let us still love a person enough to engage with them, to see if the sharing process, the laughing process, and the process of doing something different, to get something different, is something they would enjoy. No pressure, just trying to engage them, especially if you love them and have seen a brighter side of them at some point.

We get into habits that become normal for us, but not healthy for us. Being alone for too long, growing up an only child or oldest child with a long gap before the next sibling arrives, or an opposite gender sibling where sharing is not required, can cause separation behaviors. Also, if a person has lost a loved one, or is experiencing the empty nest syndrome (everyone has grown up and moved out), this type of aloneness can really affect the person who depends on being involved with others, especially their children.

When they are fighting the aloneness, they can become secretly involved in disturbing their children's lives. They try to control their lives from a distance. This interference can cause a break in the relationship if the adult child does not recognize the cause. If they do recognize it and address it with the parent, there again, is good communication. Parents should accept their new position as the "parent of an adult now", if they do not, the problem may get worse. From what I hear, parents are then consultants once children become adults. Even young adults for some.

Communication is still an important key in opening the doors of happiness and having a healthier mind, body, and spirit. But then sometimes, just sometimes silence is good. It allows you to regroup and to refresh yourself. Know that, because your mouth does not open, it does not mean that you are not actively communicating. You may just need a station break, a vocal cleansing, a mind cleansing period. A "Me time" vacation.

Mind Is Too Mental As Teeth Are Too Dental

Please, if this is the case, if you are taking a break, tell someone a least one person, so that if you are not back within a certain time, mentally or physically, someone knows when you left and where you went. You know? Tracking and checking because we care.

Healthy silence truly is golden and the value of being in peace and quiet is priceless. Challenge yourself and select a time when you will be in silence and see how that works out for you. Have that mind/mental conversation with yourself. You can write, think, eat, drink, but all in silence.

The mind is so full of thoughts, ideas, and decisions, that when we are engaged in talking, we miss some of the opportunities to capture nuggets that are coming to us. As an exercise, go into silent mode for an hour. Before you go or while you are there, write down a list of things that you have been thinking about and talking about. Leave space in between each item or write each item on different pages, so when the thoughts start coming you can fill in the space. Watch out, this could be a movie in the making….

Did you know that mind and mental have the same meaning? So, it is worth an hour, a day, a weekend, a week, or even a month of silence. To get it right? Right? Try any of these silence exercises. Try them alone or with a group of friends for 3 hours. Being together in silence, 3 hours straight. It should be interesting. Record it.

Remember Braco the Croatian Gazer, his silence is truly golden.

Keep watch for The Networking For Success, Life Retreats, including the Silence Retreat.

Mind Is Too Mental As Teeth Are Too Dental

Notes

American Sign Language (ASL)

Here we have a community where the language that is spoken is not understood in the larger community that they are living in. Much like living in a foreign country and not able to speak the native language. Members of this community are not understood as easily or at all by those who are around them. Right in their homeland, and this should change. I believe this community is so under served in terms of information and entertainment access. More should be done.

How do we reach the hearing-impaired community, a condition that can affect anyone at any time by the way? I suggest that American Sign Language or the hand language of your country to be the second language taught in all school systems. Let's get it started in the United States as soon as possible. This will serve as another form of communication, and just in case you are unable to speak verbally, or decide to stop speaking, this could be a perfect way to communicate your thoughts to others. It will also allow you to communicate in many parts of the world while on vacation, where that country uses this or a similar form of hand language. Every public form of entertainment such as news, movies, plays, comedy shows, concerts, and other organizational events, should have ASL or the native hand language interpretation available for inclusion.

The feeling of being included can improve the lives of many, making them happier and giving a greater feeling of safety. Knowing that more people can understand them, their needs and having the ability to communicate their feelings, can bring joy and peace to the inner soul. Inclusion for everyone is very important to make this a better world to live in and enjoy. The larger community that is affected by this break in communication would be the parents and friends of those who cannot hear or speak fluently. We are all in the world together, and we should learn to understand each other as best we can.

Everyone in Medical, Educational and Law Enforcement professions should have ASL training, even if basic. It's America and it is American Sign Language. Again, being the mandatory second language taught in schools, takes care of that. If you ever see it spoken, it is so beautiful to watch, even if you don't understand it. Learn at least one new language, because communication is the real key to success at whatever you choose to do in life. It benefits you, as well as others.

So here is the answer to those who say, "we are in America,

and they should learn how to speak English." Well, this is English and ASL is an American language so let's get this started.

Ready Set Go…

Learn how to sign: Youtube.com/c/learnhowtosign

Mind Is Too Mental As Teeth Are Too Dental

Notes

Cultures

There are many cultures living in the same country together. Learning something about other cultures will help us to understand why things are done a certain way, which may be different than the way you were taught.

Have you ever asked yourself, why when you are speaking to someone from another country, they look at you like they are confused? Not about you, but by what you have said to them. That is because words translate differently from country to country. As they are looking confused left eyebrow up in the air like a triple dose of Botox, just ask the question "How did you understand what I just said?" Remember your same words could have very different meanings in other cultures.

You are asking this question, not because that you are calling them stupid, but because they looked so confused. If it was not your intention to confuse them, then you should want to know that they understood what you said to them as clearly as you meant it to be understood.

You should have a person's attention when you are speaking with them or to them. This is the key to clear and effective communication. You can walk into a room and say something,

Mind Is Too Mental As Teeth Are Too Dental

then walk out under the belief that you were heard and clearly understood. When in fact, you walked into a room where people were engaged in an activity. You did not get their attention. You said something and you left the room. If what you said was not received, who would hold the blame if the directions were not carried out? You, correct.

It is important to have the attention of the person that you are speaking to, before speaking to them. Having confirmation, then moving forward confident that your mission was accomplished. In all cultures this should work.

Knowing the thoughts that you want to share is one thing but knowing that your thoughts were received with the same clarity of thought is another. This type of clarity can also be in your own culture with everyone that you speak with. To hear is one thing to understand is another. You should have people confirm what you said to them, not in your words, but what your words meant to them when they received them. Especially when giving directions on something that needs to be done.

This may seem childish, but it is the basis under which good communication was created. Imagine how much time would be wasted and conversations misunderstood, if all that is said is never received, in the way you want it to be received.

A lot. That is correct. Effective communication is essential in all aspects of life in all cultures and is one of the keys to being successful and happy. Think of some instances that you were involved in, where there were cultural differences, and the messages were not received effectively. Think of some of the same instances where that may have happened in your own culture. This could be in business or personal. What are some changes you would make for the results to be different?

Mind Is Too Mental As Teeth Are Too Dental

Notes

Notes

Mind Is Too Mental As Teeth Are Too Dental

Notes

Body Language

Watching a person's body movements is just as important as listening to what they are saying. Body language can be the tell all, to how you are feeling. Whether you are relaxed and comfortable or nervous and tense. Your position of sitting or standing, how you walk, hold your arms, or cross your legs.

These body positions and movements can tell others a lot about you, without you saying a word. When someone is speaking to you, do they have your attention or is your head up in the air? Are you looking behind you or are you playing with something in your hands, huffing and puffing like you cannot wait until this talk thing is over?

Or when someone is speaking to you, are you relaxed and focused on what they are saying? Are you hearing and listening to them carefully? Are you taking mental notes just in case you have questions? Are you giving gestures indicating to them that they have your attention, by responding with smile or nod? These are good body positions and body language indicators, showing you, as an attentive listener.

Communication is the key to success in all areas of life. Success is not measured by money alone. It is also measured, by results. Happiness and joy, which can be the result of how effective communication with others in your life, can measure your success and theirs as well.

How we influence others should be of concern to us. We must learn how to use all the tools that are available to us. Whether it is about something good or not so good in our lives. Even when information is being delivered, having the proper tools will be key to getting the job done correctly. Think of these ideas as mental and physical tools for the stage that you are building, for this act in the play of your life.

Choices that we make daily can affect our lives today and our futures. They can affect the lives of others. Think long term when making decisions about your life. Be willing to modify your plans, not because of failure, but because we as humans are continuing to develop in our lives as we grow older and wiser, and as we gather more experiences. Choices are ours to make.

How we position our bodies and the movements that we make when someone is speaking to us can determine the speaker's response. The reactions that we give to certain words, can let the speaker know how well we are receiving and understanding their information. This is even true in self-defense movements. The eyes and the stance will let the opponent know your next move. However, you can use that action to protect your next move as well.

If you are sharing your plan of change with someone and their body language shows that they are uncomfortable with the conversation, you may want to pause. Think about what you have said, and the way it was said. As you evaluate what was said, you may realize that something needs to be changed in your plan. A sign from above. Or it is possible that the listener does not agree with what you are saying, so a confused look is another possible reason for pause. It gives you time to decide whether you should continue with this conversation. It also gives the listener a chance to question what you have said or opt out of the conversation. Especially if they do not agree with the direction of the conversation.

We are learning everyday something new, and that something can stimulate another thought which can affect your initial plan. What should you do now? You can take this time to re-evaluate your short and long-term plans and see how the "new" thing fits in. You may also see if the changes that you are considering, are on track for your continued happiness. If we are here in this life, on this earth, changes are going to happen.

Stay prepared for changes. Watch and listen carefully to evaluate the experiences and lessons of your actions as well as the lessons and actions of others.

Talk extensively to the older and sometimes wiser people that you know, or those who you meet along the way. Watch their body language. See how comfortable they are talking with you. Watch how their eyes light up, excited to be asked and engaged again. Our Elders have so much to share, from history, to the present and their visions of the future. We are at a point in our lives where listening is going to be most important, to understanding the directions of our tomorrows.

Talk to the children. Ask their opinions on certain situations that you may be going through. Children are so knowledgeable and informative. See how their body language communicates with you. Watch their expressions and feel their feelings. See if they are comfortable and confident in what is being shared. We can learn so much from them, if we just ask and listen. Then when they turn to us to talk, we should do the same. Listen and ask questions. Keep your body position and movements in check. They can sense if you are not really listening to them.

Children of all ages have a lot to share. They have been given detailed instructions and information that is very useful to adults and to their own futures. Forget their age recognize their value. If you question their knowledge because of their age and what you believe they should and should not know, here's a test. Give them a technology device and see what they can do with it. Please don't be too surprised when they know how to operate it better than you. Ask them a question which would require experience and see how they respond. Careful you may want to be seated for this one. Knowledge is universal.

Watch and listen to the body language of those around you. Say nothing, see everything. You will know the gist of the conversation and how attentive everyone is listening, just by watching their body language. You can even feel the energy of the conversation by watching the body's movements. Just watch and listen with your eyes.

Mind Is Too Mental As Teeth Are Too Dental

Notes

Mind Is Too Mental As Teeth Are Too Dental

Notes

Mind Is Too Mental As Teeth Are Too Dental

Notes

Creative Writing

What a joy it is to pick up a writing tool and just start writing. Doodling is a habit of many writers in the making. Jotting notes here and there, then when you least expect it, you have a completed project. The sky is not the limit. As we have come to learn. We have no limits in our ability to succeed.

Writing allows for thoughts received to pass through our brains to be displayed on paper or screen. This can be for us alone or to be shared with others. Our writings can come to life. They can be turned into books, plays or movies. One of the greatest things that can come out of writing notes, are great stories. Some true, some not so true. Even as fantasy, (there's that daydreaming again), which can easily become reality. That's when art begins to imitate life.

How is writing good for helping people to cope with life's issues? When expressing yourself in a letter to someone that you care about, it helps you to get your thoughts and feelings out without interruption. Journalizing your thoughts, dietary intake, daily activities, and weekly plans helps to keep you on track of what you want to accomplish. Writing keeps the mind working and that is good. It keeps the mind in creative mode. It

Mind Is Too Mental As Teeth Are Too Dental

is also a good exercise for the hands. Practice… Practice… Practice…

If you are creatively dictating, that's great for speech therapy. Especially for those in need of speech therapy. Dictating and singing the thoughts can help those who may have had a stroke or other condition which affects their speech. Singing comes from the right side of the brain, which is the creative side, not the left logical and analytical side. So, practice creative dictation to a melody. Sing on. Be as creative as you would like to be and see what comes from it.

If you are hearing voices, write down what they are saying. Sometimes it is your creative side expressing ideas for productions. Once you see those messages outside of your mind, you may begin to understand them better. People are often afraid of the voices, based on what we have been told. Explore options of controlling them, and not letting them control you.

Understanding the messages, allows time to figure out what is really being said. They could be providing self-therapy, to help you with life situations. Learning to control those conversations, gives you more control over them. Analyzing yourself in the process is very therapeutic. If you begin to journalize your life experiences, you may find an award-winning play, movie, or book, just waiting for you or someone to create, if you share.

Remember some people get ideas and others bring them to life. These ideas are good lessons for the receiver and the larger community, as we are to share with others what we are going through. Again, it may not be your lesson, though you may be in the midst of the receiver, therefore you get it also. Everyone who gets the lesson can deliver it to others who may need it. Teamwork.

Writing a lot can also improve your penmanship, which may improve your self-esteem. How well your handwriting is, can determine your success in certain positions in life. One good point to mention is that everything about us can always improve. We are forever becoming who we are supposed to be. We should always be in learning mode. Trying this and trying that. Everything about us can always improve. It happens with practice. So, stay aware and follow the signs.

Writing down your thoughts, plans and past actions is therapy especially when you review it. Practice equals activity and activity happens with understanding that, the more we do, the more we know and grow. Let's practice being happier in our lives and sharing our happiness formula with others. One person at a time.

Communication is the key!

"Communication It Is Your Turn"

"Suicide...Be Gone, Take Sadness, Depression, Personality Disorders, Chemical Imbalances, Fear and Loneliness With You! Please and Thank You!"

List some ways that you feel creative writing and effective communication can improve any type of relationship, hence life.

Mind Is Too Mental As Teeth Are Too Dental

Notes

Mind Is Too Mental As Teeth Are Too Dental

Notes

Mind Is Too Mental As Teeth Are Too Dental

Notes

Notes From The Writer/Co-Author!

Evadynè Smith

"I Thank You Very Much For Reading This Book"

I hope that it will help you or someone that you know live a happier and healthier life. When you make the decision that you need a life change, it is not the end of your life, but the end of a life you have lived already. There are so many ways to make changes. I hope you found a way through these pages.

I was led to comment about suicide and mind/mental health on social media when we received the news that Robin Williams committed suicide. I knew that Robin had a group of professionals that He could see and speak to when He wanted or needed to. Robin was the closest to me, with a reported suicide death.

With so many other high-profile suicides being reported since then, in the height of their careers with so many plans literally on table and then gone, this became a crisis for me! These reports were coming to often. This was going from bad to worse. Growing too popular. Being to accept, with no further investigations as to IF and WHY?

Mind Is Too Mental As Teeth Are Too Dental

A thought came to me that something else needed to be done to change this pattern of acceptance. I decided to write a book because there was, and is, a need for more clarity, to demystify it and to understand some of the causes. At the same time and with the level of importance and urgency, is learning the ways of preventing suicides and suicidal thoughts and mind/mental health conditions that are sometimes preventable.

Just because something has happened or a diagnosis or illness has you burdened, should death be the answer? The more you know, the better the outcome. The diagnosis could be wrong. The prognosis could be wrong. We are all individuals, and the cookie could be cut just a little different in our case.

Just because someone may have a mind/mental or emotional health condition, does this justify accepting the cause of death as an intentional suicide. The accessories often play a role in the act. Right?

I felt that I needed to add something to the solution puzzle. The original titled book, Suicide Is A Serious Killer, Let's End It Today", (the baked potato) was released in 2018 with 78 pages, self-published, thankfully, because although the messages were there and clear, so were the many typos. Then released again about 176 pages, still a few typos but with more powerful messages and information. The readers loved the content, and it helped so many people open up conversations and feel better about life. The final edition, over 300 pages with blanks pages for notes. That was to treat you not to cheat you...lol, and with over 41000 words. Please use those note pages wisely.

Though received well, the word suicide seems to be synonymous with fear, evil, satan, anti-religion, shame, mind/mental health, selfish and coward. Who knew that people feared knowledge, feared understanding, was ashamed to learn that someone who they loved so hard, could quickly, without planning, end their life, but not because they wanted to. To learn that their life, that was looking "so good and living so full" came to an abrupt stop, because of protein deficiency, a chemical imbalance, a misfiring of the brain connectors. Not unhappiness. That's why I began to look for a softer, more welcoming title for the next book, that would be made from the first, but included some ingredients for a milder taste.

That would be this book that I call, "the potato salad", made from the hot baked potato. It was needed because I felt that a softer title and approach would allow people to not be afraid of the book. They would open it and read it. I was thinking about

Mind Is Too Mental As Teeth Are Too Dental

a title, and kept hearing, "it's right in front of your face". I questioned, "what's right in front of my face?" This went on for four days, back and forth, until one day when I was speaking with someone and again said, "mind is too mental as teeth are too dental, and we all have a mind". When I looked at the persons facial expression, that had a smile and they said, "yes that make sense", I was like, OMG, that is what was right in front of my face…the acceptance and realization of the statement. shown in the expressions of many peoples faces that I had spoken with over time, when talking about the book. This was in late November 2022. A title that would be softer, more inviting and waa laa. Oh, did I mention that this four-day talk was in my mind. The back and forth, Q&A that I kept hearing, the, "it's right in front of your face" and the "what's right in front of my face" talk. That's right! That kind of conversation and realization, of "talking to yourself", working it out… But what's funny is, on October 23rd, I recorded a video that's on my YouTube (@evadynesmith3986, titled "Mind Is Too Mental as Teeth Are Too Dental". Just saying….

That's where this title came from. It was an Ahhh haa moment, and yes much of the book is the same. A few things added and not to fool you, just to get the message across that, we just.

cannot accept a statement as fact, when there are so many factors that may have contributed to the act of self-harm, if it was, and mind/mental conditions. The state of our lives is so important. So many acts to our play of life.

Make this book personal to you. Use the note pages for your thoughts about those who you know, who may benefit from at least 400 words between these pages. I sincerely hope these pages fit into the puzzle of the lives that need changing and saving on so many levels, including the Victims of Loves Lost.

I am a Messenger at Large. Sharing what I receive to benefit others. Every day is a new day, a new beginning and new ideas come. Using what you have learned along the way and having the time to make different decisions about life, is a blessing. Someone always has more or less than we have, but it is the joy that we can find in what we have, and what we can achieve that will truly matter in our lives.

The happiness that we find in ourselves, will allow us to be happy for others. Appreciating what they have acquired for themselves is good and encouraging. We should be inspired by these accomplishments and not feel competitive. Life is not about competition. We all have our own journey to travel and our own pearls to gather. Watch "Intimidation or Inspiration" on my Youtube @evadynesmith3986

Do not let any of the agents block your joy or happiness. Instead find your joy and your happiness inside. It is in there, and if it is just one thing that brings you to a happy thought and leads you to have good feelings then…LET THAT ONE THING GROW TALLER, THAN THE CLOUDS!

It is especially important that we look at trends and customs and how they began. Once on a roll people begin to believe without question that these behaviors and practices are "normal" and for "everyone". Try to research the origin of what is given as, "the thing to do", or "what is expected of you." Ask where did all of this come from? Whose idea was it to make it a fact, a thing, an expectation, for all to follow? Under what or whose "reign" did this idea launch?

There is a trend that causes suicide and mind/mental health to be a hush hush don't talk about it, mysterious subject, not to be discussed. Well, if not discussed as we discuss every other form of illness or death, then how will we ever be able to understand their causes, capture them, then conquer them?

I was overhearing the lyrics of a song saying, "my friends are all dead take me to the edge." I was like WHAT! That sounded to me like an invitation for death to come. That is unacceptable if so. These lyrics could plant an idea into the minds of those who are listening, subliminally, whether they know it or not. I hear there is a new term for suicidal thoughts called "intrusive thoughts". Still afraid of the word, like it will bring the action.

Still, no one is giving a clear explanation as to why these thoughts come, or what they would sound like. Until now. They are only advising people to ignore them.

As casually as we see they can enter the mind, "just ignore them." Really?

With so many reported suicides, self-harm incident, with no pre-existing conditions, it will take a bit more information about these agents, and the thoughts, than just "ignore them". Obviously, that alone is not working. There are people passing on by way of suicide who are successful, happy on the outside and who were living a luxury life from what we can see. They had all that they needed within their reach and more coming, but then something happened.

What happened to trigger this thought, is the real question. What would lead them to want to end their lives? Some are under professional care, and some have no know mind/mental or emotional health conditions at all.

Was it protein deficiencies caused by lack of proper nutrition or from the side effects of medications prescribed for a health condition, if they had one? Was it street drugs or alcohol taken or tainted with or without their knowledge? Was it a subliminal suggestion and then a trigger, to set it off? What caused the intrusive, destructive, harmful, homicidal, and suicidal thoughts that led to the life ending or attempted action? What?

There are happy people living in comfortable positions, then gone. Children who are happy and doing well in school, from happy homes. They love playing with their friends, and then they decide to end their young lives. These instances made me think hmmm...what could have gone wrong? Did they watch something from a media source or listen to a song, get a phone call, or text message that triggered an action that may have been planted in their minds?

What? What? What? and Why? Are always the questions when this action happens. Some survivors don't know why they attempted to end their lives. A thought or action and no pre-existing concerns. I met a very nice Lady; Debra R and we were talking about suicide. I mentioned to her the casual way it creeps in and many people don't know where it comes from. I shared with her that in the book, I suggest talking with a survivor, as the why question. If they say they don't know, I said believe them. She was totally shocked; the hairs were standing up on her arms. She shared that she had a dream 2 days before, where a young man took his life, then looked at her and said, "I don't know why I did it". It was a reason that we met, to have that conversation and to confirm some of what is in these pages.

When survivors say they don't know why they did it, believe them, and try to help them understand, it may not have been their idea. Explain that chemical imbalances causes the body's neurotransmitters to miscommunicate in the brain. The effect of this miscommunication can result in many things from within our bodies.

Watch "Brain on Fire" online.

You have everything and more. You appear happy. Family is doing well. You may be experiencing challenges, at work, home, friends, and peer pressures from anywhere. Maybe you are using or have used street drugs and alcohol on occasion, which can affect you long after you have stopped using them. These things could be factors as to why you may need to change your life. But changing it, is not ending it. Instead, change is making it different. Doing something different.

Who is helping you with these issues, problems, or concerns? Who are you talking to or with if these agents can get the upper hand? What are they talking about? Who else are they speaking to, about you? Is it anyone who you know, and who really knows you? What are they saying to them?

Or are they reading from a manual following other people's instructions? Are they making decisions about you based on a theory process or through information from a book? Generalizing, what if it is this or what if it is that? Do they know how to get to the root of the issue?

Then there are the nutritional medicinal and chemical causes that can take place in our bodies which can be the root of having sadness, depression, suicidal thoughts, and now we have learned homicidal thoughts as well. There are medications, the ones advertised that can cause sadness, depression, and suicidal thoughts. But what about the combination of medications? What are the internal effects on a person's mind and body who is taking more than one, like three, four, five, six, or seven in a day? Are there studies on the combined drug interactions? I met a Lady Helen, who said her husband was on 30 different daily medications. Keep protein in your diet, and often drink a detox tea for your kidneys and liver.

People have horror nightmares from high blood pressure medications who do not engage in watching media content of that sought. This is the time to talk about what you are feeling and experiencing. Nightmares and high blood pressure, hmmm..., sounds a bit deadly to me. In your sleep? Not so peaceful, huh? The side effects can affect you more seriously than the condition that you have.

Again, the example of the Lady who is a dialysis patient, driving her car hearing FASTER, FASTER, FASTER, NOW CRASH. She thankfully, is a woman in her right mind, without issues of life pressing on her shoulders. If she had these pressures, she may have followed those directions. Her mind was very capable of knowing right from wrong. She knew that idea, was very wrong. When she investigated her new medication for dialysis support and saw that one of the side effects read, "can cause suicidal thoughts" she was relieved and shocked at the same time.

We hear or read this in the commercials for medications. But when are we told what those thoughts would sound like? When do we ask ourselves, "what would those thoughts sound like?" No one mentions, "what those thoughts would sound like." No one gives examples of suicidal thoughts, so when they come, they are unexpected and all too familiar. You don't even realize that it happened, in that way. So casually. Hmm...

That's what hush hush will get you. Let's not tell too much about what happened. Ssshhh...It may come our way. Let's not mention, to the public how this happened. We'll pretend it was in their sleep. But guess what? Talk or not, if you don't know how it looks, how it sounds and what can cause it, you may be surprised as well, if it happens to you or a loved one.

Understand that a person may not be going through any emotional trauma, and it could be creeping up and just waiting for that opportune time to jump out and attack. As with all mind/mental health conditions, a gradual onset of behaviors, that may look normal for that person, and others may say, "oh that's just their way". But in fact, it's a condition that is graduating to something more serious.

I remember back in the 70's, in the 1970's, I should be clearer, because I do not know when you are reading this. It could be the year 2097 and if so, I sure hope that all these books that I am writing, become a part of history. History that says, "those books, by that lady Evadyne`, change my life, or the lives of many in our society." That these books have become some of the most effective thought provoking and influential pieces of literature that slowed down or ended people passing, by way of circumstantial suicide. That these books helped people with undiagnosed medical and mind/mental health conditions. Also, that they are the most popular pieces of literature that led more people to living a happier and more fulfilled life. Fairytales with happy endings. "JUST SAYING."

I sincerely hope the agents affecting people's peace of mind and happiness, are subjects of what use to be, and not what is. I hope these conditions and issues have ended long before the year 2097. Therefore, if you are reading this book or any book that improves understanding life, health, and nutrition, at any time, in any year, please be a part of the change. Share the books and help make this information a successful piece of the human survival packet. As the world is rapidly changing, we need all the survival tools available, to keep living and living happily. Let's Go!

So back to my thoughts…in the 1970's when I was young, and I would hear of people committing suicide, it was by way of the oven, their wrists, pills, or drowning. After hearing the examples within these pages, I now, in the early 2020's, am wondering if the oven was when they were lighting the pilot light, which use to go out often, and this sneaky sneak suggested a couple of deep breaths. Or when peeling potatoes, the sneaky sneak suggested the wrist. Or how about the pills, which are usually prescribed to the victim. Maybe while taking them this sneaky sneak says… oh how colorful…mix them up and take more and more.

Drowning? Well, everyone takes a bath at some point in their life. What if this thing gave directions that seemed simple and relaxing but ended in death. Now that we know how sneaky it could be. How about that? Casually speaking. Yuk! No pre-existing feelings of emotional distress to the point of ending life. Maybe there could have been protein deficiencies in the body causing the neurotransmitters to malfunction. Or it could be caused by the side effects of medications or natural nutritional or chemical imbalance, allowing these agents to enter and control the thoughts and actions of the person. Short term and long term.

These situations can cause the brain to think and act opposite of what the person may want to do. Especially if they are experiencing any of life's challenges. Mind control from the internal technology in the body.

Yes, we are electrical beings. Right? And with that, electrical communication is ongoing. Right? That's how we learn how to read, write, eat, walk, talk, type, sing, dance, calculate with our minds, we think and pull thoughts to make ideas, get shocked by certain fabrics or watch our hair follow the comb or brush when held above without it touching. Just to name a few electrical, technical attributes that we are capable of. Have you ever heard something or watched something and felt the hairs on your arms stand up? Yes, we are electrical beings. So, there we have it, Technology 101.

Then there are the implants that are medically installed for specified health reasons. Right? Technology 102. What? You ask. Some of the technology in people with implants, transplants, cardiac instruments, dental materials, hearing devices again, just to name a few, transmit and receive signals.

Mind Is Too Mental As Teeth Are Too Dental

Many of these items can pick up signals and sounds that can cause mind altering affects. Hearing sounds out of nowhere...hmmm. Research some neurological tests that are performed on children to determine ADHD as an example, and how the test can be "manipulated" for the needed results.

Veterans and other people are living with bullets, metal plates and other foreign objects in their bodies. Bullets could cause lead poisoning, which effects are mostly discussed regarding lead paint and children. However, brain development issues, with "adults', the big children with brains and other body parts, can be negatively affected by metal toxicity as well?

What are the adult and child health risks or conditions based on toxic levels of lead, aluminum, cadmium, plastic, and mercury poisoning? Which by the way, lead and other metals are in food products, tattoo ink, deodorants, lotions, and cosmetics etc.

What are the long-term effects of these elements in the body, and how does medications conflict with these conditions? Look it up! I did. Alzheimer's, Parkinson's, Dementia, Anemia, Cancers, and Auto Immune diseases, just to name a few. Then there are the external sources of mind control, the media, misguided professionals, video games, movies and music which can all lead to bad actions resulting in hurt and pain.

Communicate Your Feelings to Someone Please! Do not be afraid that because you share what's going on in your life, someone will label or misunderstand you. If that happens shrug it off, because people will do what they know how to do. You don't have to let it stop your process of releasing your feelings. Find someone else to speak with, who will respect what you are doing and saying. Let it out because it's what you need to do. A toe label would be much worse than any other label from someone with limited knowledge of how to be kind, respectful and a good listener.

Join our "Group Therapy" meeting on Zoom Sundays at 12 noon est. It's People Helping People. You can join and ask questions, or you can email your concerns and we the People offer suggestions: TeamFollowMe@yahoo.com Subject: GroupTherapy or GT Also join "Evadyne` with Company, Talk Worth Listening Too" Podcast on most podcast networks, Call in Mondays 4pm-6pm est and join the Talk: 520-525-8633.

People are committing suicide and their reason is because their friend or a loved one did the same thing. Well,

some of these people have children and families. Would they expect their children and loved ones to follow them? I sure hope not. "Don't Forget To Say Goodbye", Chapter 9, may help a person find their true value and their direction to stay here with other loved ones.

These acts may have been influenced by the accessories, drugs, prescription and non-prescription, protein deficiencies, chemical reactions, chemical imbalances, or suggestions from trusted people to act in this way. Something else needs to be done, for people who unknowingly are attempting this act and for those who are intentionally considering ending their life, the life they now know. They need to know there are other options.

I had a view on people choosing to leave this life by means of suicide, which was, "if you are ready, then okay." If you felt that you had fulfilled your purpose, and want to leave, just "don't forget to say goodbye." At the time I did not realize that ready may not have been by their own decision. I did not agree with departing without conversations with loved ones. I did not feel that it was fair to leave such empty holes full of questions, and to leave in such trauma, drama ways.

Realize that leaving this life does not have to mean by way of death. Changes can be made by shifting gears and exploring new areas to live in and new things to do. Chapter 6 Transformation…The Change, decision making and living on. Welcoming different experiences, while looking forward to having another adventure or maybe a first real adventure. Having no real adventures in life could be the reason for deciding to end it. Just go have an adventure. Permission granted!

Make plans to live the life that you feel you want to live and begin today. Imagine that!

I know, you will find people who will not agree with your decision to change or your process of starting your transformation. They may need time to process it more themselves, or they may be selfish. There may also be a level of fear of embarrassment, based on the comments from friends, parents, family members, regarding your decisions. Those who will look for blame and to blame others. But guess what, do what you must do, to make yourself happy. They will still be here.

Mind Is Too Mental As Teeth Are Too Dental

These same people, until they learn more about life and living happy, will have the same comments if these agents win, over change. What we should do is show love and support for the person who is changing. Love should outweigh all things, to keep you and your loved ones safe. One should take the time to hear and listen carefully to the reasons why this person who desires the change, desires it. It's personal first and others second.

Marriage "Till death us do part" is a strong statement. I and others take words seriously. I do not say those words for these reasons:

1. Because life is long, as it should be, and development continues. People sometimes grow apart. Not the love but the mutual interests, compatibility, and/or their long-term goals. What do you do now? Make changes and shift gears. Communicate the new feelings and desires, and sometimes the talk may change the whole picture. Listen to or read the lyrics of the song that I use to call the Pina Colada song, it is called "Escape" by Rupert Holmes. I now use this as the starter for couples and marriage counseling sessions. It makes you smile when you understand the words to this song.

2. Then there is the harsh act of murder/suicide. You see, people do take those words to heart, so when change happens, that kind of closeness and commitment is one that can lead to murder/suicide. For better or worse. The "till death us do part" statement, well people stick to those words till the end. There is the chemical reaction that can cause mind/mental health problems, that can make people do the unthinkable. Emotional explosions can happen when the other person is not ready to end the relationship.

Love someone enough to want their happiness as much as you want yours. Despite the inconveniences it may cause. Be willing to love someone from afar, as you loved them in the beginning. Be their friend until the end and support their living changes.

If any of these agents get their way, a greater inconvenience, sad feelings, confusion, and a great loss will occur. Keep in mind the other accessory story that caused homicidal thoughts. Those thoughts are as real, as the sadness, depression, and suicidal thoughts. Watch "How To Have A Happy Relationship", "How To Have A Happy Divorce" and "When A Relationship Loses It's Sizzle" on my YouTube @evadynesmith3986. It's all about life and being happy.

Mind Is Too Mental As Teeth Are Too Dental

So much to remember...but all is important.

This is the homicidal thoughts story again. A retired Emergency Medical Technician was in the hospital and the nurses gave him his medications. He questioned them and asked, "what did you give me"? They just looked at him and continued talking to each other. He became irate and louder and asked the same question again. They look at him laughing and casually asked, "why are they giving you suicidal thoughts?" Well, his medications was giving him homicidal thoughts, telling him to pick up the scissors and stab the nurses. When he told them that, they were shocked and immediately called the doctor.

As he told me this story he was still upset at the effect of the medications and the reaction of these nurses who seem to have felt that the suicidal thoughts were normal expected and acceptable. He is a Retired Emergency Medical Technician (EMT) who treated many people in crisis.

I wanted to demystify suicide and give an understanding of suicide from my human perspective and my insight. We can talk about the problems in our society, or we can do something to affect change. I put forth my effort to provide a piece to the solution puzzle. Not just to suicide but to understanding other mind/mental health issues, and how we are impacting each other daily.

Especially our young people and our Seniors. Ending one's life, is happening too often and more often than we know, and not intentionally. Something should be done, by all of us, to help end this cycle. We must build an awareness of these agents before they strike. We must demystify mind/mental health, so that people are not afraid to talk about it. This is not a God or Satan issue; they have their own fight. This is a human right to educate and elevate each other with knowledge issue.

We must know that it is not always the intention of the person or a result of emotional distress. The medications that are meant to manage health conditions, can create thoughts and feelings of suicide, sadness, depression, and homicide. We must also be aware of the ways it can enter the mind, so that we may prevent, guard, and close those gates. Let us do more talking and have more positive actions when it comes to changing lives, mines, yours, and those who we love. Together we can set new standards for living happier and more fulfilled lives.

Mind Is Too Mental As Teeth Are Too Dental

Children lose their parents and siblings and even their friends on the playground, and we move on like, they will get over it. Not always the case. They are not adults, who may have a bit more experience with loss. We must protect them, prepare them, and love them even more. For children, any kind of loss is painful, devastating and can have long lasting effects on their happiness. This is true whether it is a person, a pet, or a loved toy. It could even be their comfort place, like their home, or school, where many children experience love and care. We up and move them to relocate for financial or safety reasons, not considering the effect it will have on the child's life. Children are important in the decisions we make in life. Watch "13 Reasons Why" Season 1 online. All actions will result in reactions. Communication is key.

Playing some video games, children and adults alike are becoming desensitized not only to death, but also to rape, suicides, bullying, and murder. But even if the child plays these games, know that in real life, loss is something to talk about. Do know that children of all ages should be embraced, because when children are older in their adult life, their childhood experiences will still affect the results of how well they will live.

We see every day that life goes on after loss. Not the same of course, but for those who stay steadfast in it, life will go on. Let us start preparing the young and old for the passing on process. Start having the conversation about, "when I am no longer here", or what do you want me to do when you pass on? Passing on is a part of life. We have no actual date on our calendars; however, we all know that it is coming. What do we do? Prepare the living to be okay and not to rush into any decisions. You can even pre-arrange services for yourself, so that everything is as you want it to be. No misunderstandings and emotional spending, which can happen out of love.

Also, we do not want to rush it. HUH? You ask? Well, yes. The new conversation between medical professionals and patients, who have chronic or critical illnesses, goes like this; "well if it gets to the point where we can do nothing else for you, would you like for us to help you comfortably transition?"

Did you know? Yes, this is the conversation that allows the Physicians to enter another role. Odd Dr. Kevorkian was jailed for the same thing. My, how times have changed. Please remember, if a person wanted to pass on, before old age, they would not agree to treatments that offered living longer. Instead of helping you get better, the 3rd party entities are not allowing Physicians to do what is needed from the start of the condition in many cases. So now at the point when, "we can't help you any further", comes along, at the end of their procedural scope of services, "let us help you out," like out, out? "Literally out?" is their only next step.

Why would a person say yes to this? Because at that time, with the patient's condition and state of mind, and their amount of faith in medicine, what the Physician is now offering seems acceptable. Now that you know a little more, ask these questions; "In terms of my care and the plan of treatment, what is my projected outcome? Ask, "how has this care plan helped to improve the quality of life and extension of life for others with the same condition?" Get to know the medicine/medical business a little better. Being an educated consumer is the best way to be a great, healthy, and living customer.

Regarding preparation for passing on, I would call my Mother every day to talk, making sure she was awake, seeing how she was doing, chatting a bit, when one day I asked her "So Ma, what do you want me to do when you aren't here, when you pass on." She said, "Put me away in my red suit." We met that request halfway. She was laid to rest in red and blue and she was as beautiful as always. It wasn't a hard question for me to ask, and for her to answer, because it is the inevitable result of living.

We all should do our best to prevent any kind of untimely and unnecessary loss of life. I add these few pieces of information to the solution puzzle, in hopes that more people will come to understand it better. To openly have conversations about feelings and life in general. There are people who take a position and blame the victim of a reported self-inflicted death. Calling them selfish, wanting to punish them. These same people also chose not to attend their services. This is due in part to not understanding the real why and how the person was led to the action. Everything isn't as it seems, even with evidence including notes.

There are people who start blaming the evil spirit, the ungodly spirit. Which is also why this subject is a touchy, hush, hush subject. Their decision to blame the victim, is based on their religious teachings and who wants to challenge that? Hopefully more has been learned about suicides, mind/mental health and addictions, through these pages and further conversations will be had, for more understanding.

Suicidal actions is a touchy subject? Taboo? The "do not talk about it subject? Could this be because it leaves such big "empty" holes full of questions, that no one can or want to answer. Maybe on a personal level, someone close has been affected by it and that would make it an emotional conversation to have. I believe that should make it a needed conversation, especially if it has affected someone close. We do not want it to happen again. Do we? Let's talk about all types of mind/mental health conditions and keep learning more about how to recognize if someone is dealing with a mind/mental health condition, that needs assistance.

Because again, we all have a mind, and the state of our minds vary day to day. The mental state can be fantastic, enthusiastic, euphoric, happy, great, good, not so good, today, and in need of assistance.

Let us stop these suicides and self-harm activities, by disarming them, taking away the mystery of it. Let's stand and face it head on with a true commitment of having open communication, understanding, love, compassion and sharing with honesty, life's situations that come upon us.

This also means sharing experiences with others to empower them, should in case they are faced with the same situations.

Why let someone stumble if you know the rock is there? Give them a heads up…and a better chance of success. Hmmm…Humanity 101

You will hear people say, "let them learn the way I learned," which really means, they have not learned enough. Each One Teach One! That is the real lesson in life. Learning is an important part of life. We are to learn, as long, in time, as we are to live. (t)

Communication is the key to true learning. Let us begin to communicate more. Let us see the importance of sharing information that we receive with others. We should find resources to learn how these thoughts can begin in a person's life. Learn that with early detection, open communication and eliminating tools, together we can nip this thing in the bud. As they use to say. We can do this one step at a time. That is the goal.

Here is another example of an accessory suicide or the result of mind/mental conditions: What you do not know can hurt you. Hospital, DNR and what it really means. DNR "Do Not Resuscitate" Well guess what? Please get a full understanding of what that really means. I know some people who misunderstood. They stated, "I don't want to be hooked up to machines." Some have passed, due to lack of knowledge and understanding that some machines keep you alive and healing.

DNR is total! Finished! Do not do ANYTHING to save my life! NOTHING! However, understand there is a difference in life saving machines that can assist you to get better, and machines that are keeping you alive, with no hope of recovery. So be clear on what you want and do not want because in the end, it could mean life or death.

Visit my YouTube.om/@evadynesmith3986 and the website www.NetworkingForSuccess.info for additional information. Check out the conversations about life and the things we should know, on the talk series Evadyne` with Company Talk Worth Listening Too…

I remember hearing news reports about parents killing their children and saying, "there was too much pressure." Family members and friends in shock and saying, "they should have said something; I would have taken the children."

So now, if that should happen in the future, someone comes to you and say they are overwhelmed and need a break, do not judge them, instead, HEAR, LISTEN, and UNDERSTAND their cry. If you cannot take the children find someone "now" who would be available just in case, you get the call.

If your child or teenager is going through something like puberty, which we all should know, can cause a lifetime of hormonal crisis, keep an eye on them, even before that expected puberty age. We do not know when that age is any more, with all the changes going on, but watch and understand that they know not what they are doing. Neither did we during that time. We all remember the "when I was your age stories."

Each generation arrives with more knowledge, energy, and direction than the previous one. Remember, our parents were told by our grandparents the same thing that we are telling our young people, "when I was your age..." Life is an ongoing pattern of love, growth, reasoning, understanding, and communication.

There are signs of changes in children that are obvious. We see the outward hair growth, hear the voice cracking, cycles starting, breasts developing. What are we not seeing? We are not seeing the force of "grown", heated fluid, shooting through their veins and their brains, giving them the ability to reason and understand, in an adult way, with attitude and force of voice. We do not see their feelings, when they are being spoken to, like they are babies, or a younger child who should know better. But we do see that attitude, as the result of those feelings, and that's what many parents are challenged by.

Without lessons on how to handle, respond and maintain a respectable relationship while they are changing into young adults, as parents we may act in ways that can create a hostile living arrangement. They are feeling sure about themselves and what they know, and we are feeling that our authority is being challenged. They then become defiant, disruptive, and defensive, because they feel that you are insulting and disrespecting them.

Then you meet them on their level, with your authority, age and position, and here we go…screaming, yelling, disrespect, discipline, slaps, and disconnection of harmony…a mountain out of a mole hill…and there it goes…respect, communication, loving guidance, care and authoritative concern out the door for years to come. Because many do not return to apologize and communicate for a better understanding of what really happened.

This young adult growing within, (hormones), looks like your child, but you feel that they are acting a bit to grown up, not their age, (hormones). However, who you see, is not who they are. They are a bit more developed than what you see. Some of those new ways that are developing within their bodies, are going to be needed and required as they continue to grow and become more responsible for themselves. They will need some of those ways to protect themselves in the streets, at school and at work.

Parents try to downplay their growth and lock it away, because they do not recognize or know how to handle what they are seeing. They are feeling disrespected and attacked by their child who is only expressing themselves, based on the chemical changes in their bodies, that they are unaware of, (hormones).

Parents may be doing more harm than good for the young person growing up. Because that attitude, that ability to reason, is needed when they are not with you, and parents forget to unlock the door. Do you see what I mean? If we give and teach respect from infancy, we will give it to everyone, with patience and understanding, no matter their age. Everyone deserves respect.

Patience is a virtuous act and allows for deliberate actions,

Mind Is Too Mental As Teeth Are Too Dental

because we took the time to think about it. Do you agree? When children and adolescents are disrespected, these feelings can cause rebellious behaviors and here is an opening for confusion, anger, and then behavioral diagnosis. These agents will find a place of entry to plant and grow and that is not what we want.

We must be observant and stay awake to all the possibilities that are out there. With technology constantly in our hands, research and find three versions of hormonal changes, and what internally they may affect. Also research the other elements that are affecting our children's development, our own development, and our future. Ask friends and family what their opinions and observations are on this matter.

Be easy and patient with people in your life. People who you encounter, especially children and senior citizens my two favorite groups. These two groups consist of those who are young, and know what they know, but are not respected for knowing, because those who think they know, feel that children are too young to know. Little do they know! Give a child your cell phone or tablet and see what "they don't know." They can work it better than you. You Know?

The other group, our Senior Citizens the older wiser knowledgeable group, taught most of us what we know. They know what they know, and they also know that they know more but are not respected for what they know, because those who think they know believe that Seniors are too old to know. But little do they know; they don't know what they should know. Again.

Once again, long before the data base was related to your current equipment, Seniors designed the data base, programmed the information network, and connected circuit boards to the main frame systems. In theory and in fact. It is their data base that we should be tapping into, to better understand this life, while we still have the pleasure and gift of their company.

OOPS again.

There are so many elements that can come into the lives of people at all ages. Be prepared, and do not get caught off guard. Know that changes are not expected or accepted easily. The reactions to changes can really be frightening, as some people are afraid of change. These changes can cause people to be defensive, destructive, and self-protective or on guard. So be careful because the punch from fear may come your way unexpectedly.

While we have time, let us become an inspiration to ourselves first, then to others. Be careful of what you say to people, because once it is said it cannot be taken back. I am sorry does not erase it from the mind. I apologize. Well that either. Also, remember apologizing means that you will not intentionally do it again. Say it and mean it!

Whatever it is that you say, you should mean. About apology. When you ask for forgiveness, that is work for the forgiver, who should not have to carry the burden of work. Acceptance? Yes. Work? No! It is the wrongdoer who should have the task of working to re-earn trust.

Thinking before speaking is a particularly good practice to put in place, and a good practice to keep in place. Also sharing this information with children may be a good idea. I am just suggesting. Practice makes perfect and we can lead by example.

If you have lost a loved one in any way, and need someone to talk to, please know that there are people who can help you. Check out the links on the resource pages and find the correct group or person to listen to you. I am truly sorry for your loss. Please find a happy space and keep it close. If I may suggest, please consider writing down your feelings on paper or journalizing your thoughts and read your notes later. Write your loved ones a letter.

Remembering them and their smiles, and the value of their life should bring a smile to your face. Imagine that they are on a work assignment, away at school, an Astronaut, or in the military and deployed. Yes, you would have an opportunity to see them or talk to them again, but time will put everything into perspective.

What is the lesson in that today? Video record yourself with messages of love and laughter and record talking with your loved ones today. They will never really go away. You will always be able to hear them, see them, and feel their spirit. So will your generations to follow. They too will be able to see and hear You forever.

Watch or listen to "Conversations with God" on the internet. Know that you must go on, to live your best life. The love shared with and for the person that has left this world, is strong enough to keep the memories with you. What a blessing that is!

Mind Is Too Mental As Teeth Are Too Dental

Let's protect our minds and hearts while communicating regularly effectively and with good purpose to all.

If you haven't figured it out…the other Co-Author is the Creator.

Evadynè

Mind Is Too Mental As Teeth Are Too Dental

Notes

Mind Is Too Mental As Teeth Are Too Dental

Notes

Notes

Mind Is Too Mental As Teeth Are Too Dental

Contact the National Suicide and Crisis Lifeline

Text or Dial 988

Veterans and Active Military Preventing Substance Abuse and Suicide: https://www.linesforlife.org/mhl/ or

Text 838255

The deaf and hard of hearing can contact the Lifeline via TTY.

Dial 711

http://www.suicidepreventionlifeline.org/ GetHelp/LifelineChat.aspx

Suicide Prevention Resource Guide

http://www.sprc.org/resources-programs/program-encourageactive-rewarding-lives-pearls

Association of Black Psychologists

http://www.abpsi.org/find-psychologists

Association of Psychiatry

www.Psychiatry.org

Thoughts on Life Moving Forward

Our minds/mental states have been focused on so much since the beginning of 2020. We are now halfway through 2023. Businesses are re-opened, new businesses have started, social injustices are still happening. Crimes against people are still happening. Natural disasters are happening. Many unexplained deaths around the world are happening, all in great numbers, and the reports keep coming. Ok things are back to what some would call "normal".

We are always faced with decisions that need to be made, based on the circumstances that arise. We must be strong. We must endure with the knowledge of "how great we are"!

I would be remiss not to include an opportunity for you to share your thoughts about the current conditions under which we are living. Current events. I would like to give You an opportunity to release your thoughts, to express your emotions, share your comments and your concerns. Make this book yours. I will share mine and give you pages to write yours. You may email me if you would like to share them with me and the public or in private. Evadyne@NetworkingForSuccess.info Call: 347-457-2769

Mind Is Too Mental As Teeth Are Too Dental

First, I would like to recognize and thank all Essential Workers First Responders and Frontline Workers for all the tireless work and hours that you put in, around the world during the Pandemic of 2020. Your sacrifice is priceless and will never be forgotten.

To Your Families you are thanked for your continued support of your loved ones through the pandemic. Know that for those who lost their lives and those who are still with us, their commitment and love for human life reflects highly of them.

Honoring and Thanking Each and Every One of the Frontline and Essential Workers and Everyone who worked and made life happen for us all.

Click or visit the links below to hear a special song written for the "Heroes."

Heroes by K.Joel Spice is the song for You.

https://networkingforsuccess.info/heroes-1

Visit: www.KJoelSpice.com

Your Thoughts

Mind Is Too Mental As Teeth Are Too Dental

Your Thoughts

Mind Is Too Mental As Teeth Are Too Dental

Your Thoughts

Mind Is Too Mental As Teeth Are Too Dental

Your Thoughts

Mind Is Too Mental As Teeth Are Too Dental

Your Thoughts

Mind Is Too Mental As Teeth Are Too Dental

Your Thoughts

The Good That We See

People are more aware of spreading germs to one another therefore, they are washing their hands more. Covering their mouths, cleaning before and after use in the public areas. People are staying safe!

Thank You.

Now that we realize the risks, we will change from street clothes to house clothes before sitting on any of the household furniture. Remove our shoes at the door. Just saying. Ask yourself and others, what are you tracking into your home? Then walking barefoot later, or your baby crawling on the floor putting their hands in their mouths. Sitting on your bed in street clothes, then laying in it to sleep and wondering why you wake up sick.

I have seen and heard of such positive things that people have been able to accomplish because of the pandemic. Home-schooling was once the unthinkable on many levels by students, parents, and many school systems. However, circumstances changed everything. The concentrated learning environment has allowed some students to excel to higher levels, to research more on their own and to better communicate with Educators. This will enhance success in college for the first-year student, because the biggest shock in the first year of college is independent learning. No more hand holding. This can also be a benefit for first jobs, where you receive your instructions and are expected follow through with them, on your own.

Many are now working remotely. Educators, as with many professionals, can spend more time with their families and enjoy watching their children's development unfold. Less commuting and more commitment to self-development, furthering educational levels for themselves, building better relationships, and spending quality time with family have improved.

Parents are taking the opportunity to watch the development of their children, have more family dinners or just dinner at home period. The dynamics of the family structure is fascinating now; where it was in, out, see you later, good day, we are together more, sharing more, eating together more, talking to and with one another more, and learning more about self and family, while making plans.

People have learned that their "jobs", their tasks at work can become their business. Some have started their own businesses with great ease and success. Who Knew? We have learned to be more creative in getting things accomplished around the house, and outside of the house with technology. Organizing closets, the furniture, our minds. Virtual meetings for work and play has become the go to for entertainment and research.

People have learned how to comb their own hair, shave themselves, manicure their own nails, and appreciate natural hair styles. This is people of all cultures and ethnicities. They have even learned and practiced with improvement, cooking skills. Taking online courses or just learning something new every week, with the internet available 24/7.

So many people have retired and with no regrets. Paid off mortgages and car loans with early withdrawals from retirement accounts with no penalties. How often did you pray to work from home or wish you had a 4-day work week?

Have you noticed that your physical body is in better shape since you have been taking care of yourself? That your skin tone is healthier? Look at how small businesses were created out of the need for delivery services. People took their work experience, their vehicles, their homes, and their survival skills and made a feast of a meal, with their creativity and business ideas. Success out of perseverance. (t) Who knew?

Making it through to brighter days should be the goal for everyone, every day. Keeping your mind in the now, not the then. Checking yourself and have trusted people checking you too. Are you planning future events? Do not stop. Know that the future is always coming. If it does not, you will not know it.

So, plan like it is coming and be happy in the process. Learning more about ourselves, our family members, and friends. Learning about making decisions and not just reacting to circumstances. Reminds me of a statement from past. "Are you a decision maker or a circumstance taker?"

Let us look at the gains that have been made and find the positive seeds to continue growing. Whenever you are reading this book, I hope that everyday gets better and brighter than the last.

Let us strive to focus on success and to see the Sun through the Clouds or feel the heat of the Sun on our bodies. Keep attracting goodness and let your actions be your guidance. Just keep searching for your diamond in the blackness of the rock. It is there, just "keep on keeping on."

Mind Is Too Mental As Teeth Are Too Dental

Your Thoughts

Mind Is Too Mental As Teeth Are Too Dental

Your Thoughts

Mind Is Too Mental As Teeth Are Too Dental

Your Thoughts

Mind Is Too Mental As Teeth Are Too Dental

Your Thoughts

Mind Is Too Mental As Teeth Are Too Dental

Your Thoughts

Mind Is Too Mental As Teeth Are Too Dental

Thank You So Much!

Mind Is Too Mental As Teeth Are Too Dental

Listen to an Audio Intro

YouTube.com/@EvadyneSmith3986 or

Leave a Comment or Review on The Books Page on Amazon or the Guest Book on the website.

Call 347-457-2769 to speak to or book the Author!

Visit the BookShelf on: www.NetworkingForSuccess.info

and see what to read or listen to next.

Authors, Writers, Illustrators, Editors, Publicists. Join the

Networking For Success BookShelf

Best Of Life To You All

Evadynè

As a special thank you, we offer you an appreciation package.

www.NFSPCN.com

Upcoming Books: "Letting Loose The Juice…A Relationship Shifter" and "Mind Health For Minors, Creating Happy Adults"

Mind Is Too Mental As Teeth Are Too Dental

Contact the National Suicide and Crisis Lifeline

Text or Dial 988

Veterans and Active Military Preventing Substance Abuse and Suicide: https://www.linesforlife.org/mhl/ or

Text 838255

The deaf and hard of hearing can contact the Lifeline via TTY.

Dial 711

http://www.suicidepreventionlifeline.org/ GetHelp/LifelineChat.aspx

Suicide Prevention Resource Guide

http://www.sprc.org/resources-programs/program-encourageactive-rewarding-lives-pearls

Association of Black Psychologists

http://www.abpsi.org/find-psychologists

Association of Psychiatry

www.Psychiatry.org

"Mind is Too Mental as Teeth are Too Dental and We All Have A Mind!"

Just A Quick Re-cap…Please Continue Your Research…

To order my books wholesale, support a sale or signing event visit: (see on the website: NetworkingForSuccess.info) or

to book Me for a speaking engagement Call: 347-457-2769 or email Teamfollowme@yahoo.com

In the book where you see the (t) those are tee shirts, sweats, caps, knapsacks, and canvas tote bags that we have available on SteadyK.com and NetworkingForSuccess.info

YouTube.com/@evadynesmith3986

Protein deficiencies causes sadness, depression, suicidal, and homicidal thoughts. "Protein Up Sadness Down!" (t)

www.BeatCancer.org Cancer Coaches

BlackMagik363 on YouTube

Dr. Majid Ali, QueenAfua.com, **Namaskar.com,** Dr. Sebi, **Dr. Gwen Scott** YahkiAwakened.com**, Dr Oz book titled "YOU" The Owner's Manual."**

Mind Is Too Mental As Teeth Are Too Dental

John Monroe "Vision Care" DrBanker.com

Jerry Hickey at InviteHealth.com

RemediesHerbShop.com

For Wellness Consultation: Reiki, Essential Oils, and Nutrition Email: <u>NabihahSharrieff46@gmail.com</u>

For Healthy Green Tea visit: Tea-For-Health.com/623

The books: Back To Eden and Where There Is No Doctor

Patrick Delves **on** FB,

Dr. Raymond Omid, Chiropractor, PremiumHolistic.com

<u>YouTube.com/@TheHealthManShow</u>

Listen to the GrownFolk Talkin Podcast: Call or text Call Me to 520-525-8633, Mute until you are asked to speak. Listen to the Full Show Line Up.

My show, "Evadyne` With Company, Talk Worth Listening Too" Mondays 4pm – 6pm est. Join the Talk!

Also Join "Group Therapy" Sundays at 12 noon on Zoom email **<u>teanfollowme@yahoo.com</u>** for the link.

Make the time to detox your body for clarity. If you are sick and taking medication, take a mild laxative and drink plenty of water to move out the waste. Starting somewhere…

Read Declutter Like A Mutha by Letha Francis

https://www.amazon.com/Declutter-Like-Mutha-Letha-Francis-ebook/dp/B084SNPDZS

Read: Poetic Reverse: A Different Education "and long I looked…then prayed to another" By Dr. Jasper Costner, Jr.

Hear his interview on my YouTube.com/@evadynesmith3986

Support organizations and businesses that are doing the work to make this world a better place. Visit: The 5org page on NetworkingForSuccess.info

Mind Is Too Mental As Teeth Are Too Dental

Thank You Again!

Mind Is Too Mental As Teeth Are Too Dental

I humbly ask our Creator to please protect our minds, bodies, hearts, souls, and spirits to be able to sustain good health and wellness.

To please give us the strength and the ability to reach out and talk to someone about our feelings, when not feeling good.

I ask that we not be afraid to share life's lessons, good and not so good, so that our experiences can be a benefit to others.

I ask that we take the time to record or write down our feelings, as a way of clearing our minds and our souls so that our bodies can remain whole.

I ask this for all humans and humankind alike.

Thank You

Evadynè

Mind Is Too Mental As Teeth Are Too Dental